Mary

**IMAGES OF THE MOTHER OF JESUS
IN JEWISH AND CHRISTIAN PERSPECTIVE**

**Jaroslav Pelikan
David Flusser
Justin Lang, O.F.M.**

Fortress Press
Minneapolis

MARY
Images of the Mother of Jesus in Jewish and Christian Perspective

First paperback edition published by Fortress Press 2005.

The essays by David Flusser and Justin Lang have been translated by Xavier John Seubert, O.F.M.

For illustration acknowledgments, see page 106.

Library of Congress Cataloging-in-Publication Data
Pelikan, Jaroslav Jan, 1923–
    [Maria. English]
    Mary : images of the mother of Jesus in Jewish and Christian perspective / Jaroslav Pelikan, David Flusser,
        Justin Lang.
        p. cm.
    ISBN 0-8006-3706-2 (alk. paper)
    1. Mary, Blessed Virgin, Saint. 2. Mary, Blessed Virgin, Saint—Art. 3. Mary, Blessed Virgin, Saint—
        Jewish interpretations. 4. Christian saints in art. I. Flusser, David, 1917–2000 II. Lang, Justin. III. Title.
    BT603.M3513 2005
    232.91—dc22
                                2004029370

The paper used in this publication meets the minimum requirements of American National Standard for Information Sciences—Permanence of Paper for Printed Library Materials, ANSI Z329.48-1984.

Manufactured in Canada
10   09   08   07   06   05   1   2   3   4   5   6   7   8   9   10

Contents

Foreword   v

Mary and Israel   *by* David Flusser   1
    The Jewish Atmosphere   5
    Mary and Jewish Martyrdom   7

The Life of Mary   *Pictorial Gallery*   13
    The Background, Birth, and Childhood of Mary   14
    Mary as a Temple Virgin, the Betrothal, the Beginning
      of Her Motherhood   15
    The Birth of the Lord   18
    The Childhood of Jesus   20
    From the Wedding in Cana to the Resurrection   22
    From the Ascension of Christ to the Crowning of Mary   25

Mary and Christian Doctrine   *by* Jaroslav Pelikan   75
    Authentication of the True Humanity of Jesus   76
    Virgin Mother   79
    Theotokos   81
    Semper virgo   83
    Immaculata   85
    Assumpta   87

Mary and Catholic Practice   *by* Justin Lang, O.F.M.   90

    Those Who Love Always Exaggerate   90

    Blessing of Heaven and Earth   92

    Contours of the Doctrinal Formulation   94

    "And Splendidly the Air"   96

    Sing and Proclaim All Days   98

    In a Thousand Images   102

Illustration Acknowledgments   106

Foreword

Hail, Mary, full of grace...

Mary, the mother of Jesus, has attracted loving devotion and avid dedication among Christians for two thousand years. A humble Jewish girl, little mentioned in the New Testament accounts of Jesus, she has nonetheless been acclaimed Mother of God and Queen of heaven, while vast cathedrals—setting into stone and glass the lofty aspiration and the skilled labor of many generations—have been dedicated to her honor. Millions invoke her name in prayer each hour.

Yet the cult of the virgin has also ignited great controversy and even antipathy. In the early centuries Christians disputed her title Mother of God. Later, especially during the late Middle Ages and the Reformation, Christians denounced a devotional focus on Mary that seemed sometimes to eclipse that of Jesus himself. Still, even the reformer Martin Luther, although often bitterly critical of the cult of saints, spoke lovingly of the figure of Mary as the holy Mother of God and an exemplar of faith.

What is it that Christians have found in devotion to Mary, and what is her enduring relevance for people of faith today? In this volume, now after two decades brought into a paperback edition, three eminent historians offer sympathetic and insightful reflections—Jewish, Protestant, and Catholic—on the historical, theological, and above all spiritual significance of the mother of Jesus and Christian regard for her. Their volume pivots around some of the most beautiful Christian images of Mary, gathered into a cycle of depictions of her life. Drawn mainly from stunning medieval altarpieces, these illustrations of events from the Gospels and popular Christian literature and legends eloquently illumine popular piety and devotion to Mary.

The chapter by the late Jewish New Testament scholar David Flusser finds the key to Mary in her Jewish identity and her embodiment of the suffering and hopes of the people Israel, poignantly and ironically pertinent in light of subsequent centuries of Jewish suffering at the hands of Christians and in our time of the Holocaust. Yale historian Jaroslav Pelikan then masterfully outlines the development of Christian conviction about Mary after the New Testament period, especially as illustrated in the plates. He shows how Mariological doctrine reflected popular piety and ultimately reflected the significance of Jesus himself and the very character of redemption. Finally, Franciscan friar Justin Lang portrays devotion to Mary, especially as it appears in the liturgical feasts, prayers, hymns, images, and legends of popular Catholicism, in its ongoing role in our personal and ecclesial search for salvation and intimacy with God.

With today's increased interest in the historical figure and religious import of the mother of Jesus, this triptych of meditations reveals something of what ordinary Christians have seen in Mary for millennia: a woman of grace who did not hesitate to surrender herself to God and to open herself to all the joy and pain that her pivotal role in redemption would entail.

—The editors

Mary and Israel

David Flusser

What I write here is to be taken as meditation of a human being who has once again been chosen and condemned to play on the Jewish fiddle in the three tones of Catholic-Protestant-Jew. But within this ecumenical prison in which I am forced to sit, no one can deny me the right to sing a proper song of praise to the Jewish Mary, even when I run the danger of being fruitfully or fearfully misunderstood by those who will pass by my golden latticework. This is not going to be a pastoral idyll on the Jewish mother Mary, for her life was certainly not idyllic—not according to the version of any confession! It is clear to me that I owe Mary a meditation and one that is independent of the dogmatic developments of the different denominations and perhaps unimpaired by dogmatic positions.

As a Jew, I find myself in a paradoxical situation in comparison to most Protestants. In connection with Mary, I am not in danger of having to react automatically with compulsive resentment. I understand how such a cramped reaction to Mary originated among the "separated brethren." There were and are even to this day many exaggerations and even blunders within the devotion to Mary. Erasmus of Rotterdam had already taken those to task who "rely more on the virgin Mother of God than on her Son" (*The Praise of Folly*, chap. 40).

The second reason for the tension in relation to Mary is the Protestant criticism of the ecclesial tradition and of the binding validity of the dogmatic decisions of the old and new councils. Protestants can all the more easily criticize devotion to Mary because they hold that the New Testament alone is binding and they find there skimpy shorings for a Mariology.

But there is a third reason for the Protestant sort of negative reaction to devotion to Mary. This reason is, at least for me, the least defensible. There developed among Protestants a long time ago an almost superstitious fear with regard to holiness and sanctification. This fear has occurred because they see the danger of an alleged holiness and sanctification turning out to be a pagan superstition. In itself, this is a justifiable attitude, but it can easily cause one to fall into the opposite extreme. One could, so to speak, be throwing out the baby with the bathwater, and authentic holiness and sanctification could fall under suspicion as a result. In the Catholic church and related churches, Mary is understood as the vessel of holiness because she is the mother of Jesus. The thoroughgoing fear of an inauthentic holiness that can lead to idol worship is the third reason so many—including many Catholics—shrink away from the high regard in which Mary is held.

For Judaism of all times and types, holiness is bound to a place and to a definite time and is called forth through a definite activity; it is an integral part of the Jewish religious system. A Jew is capable of experiencing holiness. For that reason it seems to me that a Jew does not labor under the same inhibitions in developing an appreciation for the holiness of Mary in the church which makes it difficult for many a Christian to understand the devotion to Mary that is maintained by his or her Catholic counterpart. On the other hand, I must admit that, whether one is a Jew or a non-Jew, it is not easy to develop an appreciation of the devotion to Mary when one has not been raised on it as has the Catholic child who is initiated into this devotion at its mother's breast. One should not criticize Jews or Protestants because of that.

I have simply expressed some theoretical presuppositions necessary to set the tone for developing the basic meaning and explanation of Mary. In the course of our considerations we should not forget that we are speaking of a real, actually living, Jewish woman. This fact at least should arouse in everyone a semblance of respect for the historical foundations in Mary's regard. Another theoretical consideration: both Judaism and Christianity are ways of faith whose points of departure are historical facts. And there is, as we know, no way without a starting point. For that reason, the historicity of Mary and the reality of her glory and her suffering are the foundation of her devotion among Christians. And the tragedy of this Jewish woman is an aspect of the uninterrupted way of suffering of her own people, the Jews.

As we shall see, Mary can be understood as a symbol for the church and also for her own people. But one should never forget that this woman once walked the earth—this mother of sorrows. The Mater Dolorosa is not a theological concept or an overpowering experience of the archetypal but primarily a real person who was inspired by her joy and never defeated by her unspeakable pain.

Muslims, Jews, Christians of every camp, liberals and conservatives, even atheists, all who accept the existence of Jesus, will admit that Mary, his mother, connects him with the Jewish people. In other words, the mother of Jesus was a Jewess and lived a Jewish life. And as we learn from Luke, she lived that life according to the Jewish religious tradition. I have also neither read nor heard that it has occurred to anyone that Mary could have been critical of the Jewish way of life of her time or that to some extent she did not observe the law of Moses. Whether justifiable or not, this tension was reserved for her Son. And I don't want to go into that here, because I see ever more clearly how deeply ingrained is the attitude of many Christians that there is a tension between Jesus and Judaism. The tension is an indispensable, sacred prerequisite for the Christianity of quite a few Christians—theologians and faithful.

With one very important exception, about which I will have something to say, I have also never heard it concocted that an aspect of the devotion to Mary is to believe that she in her incalculable pain and anger spoke of the Jews as God-murderers. It would apparently have been thought a profaning of the suffering of Mary to utter such an accusation. However it may be, for all those who know something of Christianity, Mary is the Jewish mother of Christ.

The mother of Jesus was called Miriam—a most typical name for a Jewish woman of that time. The name appears often in the writings of the famed Jewish historian Flavius Josephus. This was also the name of the beloved wife of the evil Herod, who, cruel as he was, finally had her executed. Friedrich Hebbel has devoted a well-known play to this tragedy. In this piece the queen is called Mariamne. This is an old mistake in transcription for the original Mariamme. Mariamme is an elegant form of Mariam. The mother of Jesus is also called this in the New Testament. At that time the name Mariam was pronounced as Miriam. Our common, contemporary form of Maria is another adaptation to Greek (and Latin). For our part, we will also continue using the name Mary for the mother of Jesus, since this form has been made venerable through long use.

We should, however, still take note of the fact that the mother of Jesus was called Miriam like so many of her Jewish contemporaries. At that time, the name was so popular because the first Miriam, the biblical sister of Moses and Aaron, had been so named. It is wonderful that the name at that time was experiencing such extensive usage. It was providential that the mother of Jesus bore the same as many Jewish women; it is a symbol of her connection with them. It is also fortunate for the reason that, as we know, it indicated Jesus' bond with his people.

And something else. In antiquity and also in the Middle Ages—among both Jews and non-Jews, for example, the Greeks—we know of many men whose wives, sisters, and mothers were nameless. In relation to Jesus himself, we know the names of the brothers of the Lord, but we only know that sisters existed. This insufficient attention to the names of women in antiquity is especially painful to me; I would very much like to know the names of Peter's mother-in-law and wife, because it is clear from the New Testament that Peter lived in an exemplary marriage. On the other hand, a proportionately large number of the names of the women who belonged to the followers of Jesus have been handed down. And other women who belonged to the oldest Christian communities are mentioned by name. This great significance of women in early Christianity is certainly to be seen in connection with the high regard Jesus himself afforded women, as we learn from the Gospels. The important position of women since Jesus throws additional clear light on the devotion of Mary in the church.

The Jewish Atmosphere

The Jewish atmosphere in which the life of Mary and the child Jesus were embedded is lovingly portrayed in Luke. This Jewish atmosphere is poetically expanded in the noncanonical gospel of James. We know today that this was written no later than the second Christian century. But let us stay with the canonical Gospel of Luke! There we read, among other things: "And when the time came for their purification according to the law of Moses, they brought him up to Jerusalem to present him . . ." (Luke 2:22-24). If we read the entire pericope in Luke, it becomes clear (what we already know) that Jesus was Mary's firstborn son. But there is another fact that follows from the whole section and that for the most part is unknown, although it has far-reaching consequences for Mariology. According to the law of Moses, the sacrifice for the firstborn male is prescribed only for those children of Israel who are not of the tribe of Levi or are not the priestly descendants of Aaron.

The Levites and Aaronic priests are expressly exempted from this obligation, and this is true for both the fathers and mothers of the firstborn child. As we learn from the New Testament, Joseph was of the line of David, and I see no reason to doubt this, as there were many who were of the Davidic dynasty. But Joseph was neither a Levite nor a priest. Mary was also not of the priestly line. In any case, her father, who is called Joachim in the *Protogospel of James*, was neither a Levite nor an Aaronic priest, or no sacrifice would have been brought for the child Jesus.

On the other hand, we learn from Luke 1:36 that Mary was related to Elizabeth, the mother of John the Baptist, and from Luke 1:5 that both parents of the Baptist—Zechariah as well as Elizabeth—belonged to the Aaronic priestly families. We don't know the exact nature of the relationship between Mary and Elizabeth, but it is certain that we may not conclude from the relationship between them that Mary's father had been an Aaronic priest. In this case, Mary would not have brought an offering for Jesus to the temple in Jerusalem. One must proceed cautiously and not give too much theological significance to the conclusion of the ancient church fathers that since Mary and Elizabeth were related, Mary was descended both from the House of David and from the priestly family of Aaron. It is quite possible that Mary, although related to Elizabeth, was not of the Aaronic line. As is often the case, it is helpful for us to employ a Jewish understanding of the facts in order to make better historical sense of the stories in the Gospels.

In the same Gospel of Luke and simultaneously with the joyful excitement of the childhood pericopes, the tragic motif of the sorrowful mother is intoned. The ancient Simeon announces to Mary in the temple of God at Jerusalem that "a sword will pierce through your own soul" (Luke 2:35). In Matthew, in another episode that is closely connected with the birth of Jesus, we also hear that heart-rending theme of the terrible suffering of the Jewish mothers whose innocent children were cruelly murdered (and this continues to happen). When King Herod learned that the Messiah was born in Bethlehem, "he sent and killed all the male children in Bethlehem and in all that region who were two years old or under" (Matt. 2:16). In my opinion, it would not be difficult to show that this story has a historical element to it. But that is not our present concern.

What is important for us is what is next said: "Then was fulfilled what was spoken by the prophet Jeremiah: 'A voice was heard in Ramah, wailing and loud lamentation, Rachel weeping for her children; she refused to be consoled, because they were no more" (Matt. 2:17-8). Rachel, the mother of the Old Covenant, is certainly depicted here as a representative figure for the perhaps millions of Jewish mothers whose little children were murdered on a mass scale and who cry and sob and will not be consoled because their beloved children are no more. In a medieval Easter play Rachel enters speaking, and at the end the children who were murdered by Herod are raised to life. In Matthew, Rachel is a symbolic figure for the suffering mother, in this case for the suffering Jewish mother. And Rachel's pain for the dead children is also symbolic of the suffering of Mary in relation to her illustrious son.

Mary and Jewish Martyrdom

I have already remarked that Mary must be seen in the context of Jewish suffering. That must naturally be pointed out to Christian readers since such an explanation will appear unusual to them. I am not role-playing a Jew here, I am one. To bolster my particular point of view, I can point to the fact that it is widely discussed among very faithful Christians who are in no way Jews that Jesus was nailed to the cross not by Jews but rather by the Roman occupation forces. This is witnessed to in the Gospels themselves, and crucifixion was a Roman death penalty. I know that many consider it inappropriate to compare the death of Jesus with the dying of others. But I cannot ignore the fact that Jesus was not the only Jew who was crucified. He suffered and died in a context of Jewish suffering and death. The inscription on the cross was a proclamation of his alleged crime. King of the Jews: with this inscription the Romans wanted to strike cruelly at the heart of the Jewish hope in the coming of salvation through the royal messiah. The crucifixion of Jesus was, among other things, a manifestation of Roman anti-Semitism, which is also indisputably documented in Roman literature. Even then anti-Semitism occasionally resulted in murder.

It is reported that as John XXIII viewed a film on Auschwitz, he said at the scene of the murdered Jews, "*Hoc est corpus Christi*" ("This is the body of Christ"). I would tend to view this report as historical because the words, spoken intuitively, express a good and deep—almost primordially deep—Christology. Each martyrdom—including the unspeakably terrible recent Jewish martyrdom—is a part of Christ's death on the cross. This aspect of the *corpus mysticum*—of the mystical body of Christ—should be forgotten. And it requires of us all, both Christians and non-Christians, that we engage in a productive process of discernment.

I hope I have shown how the cross of Jesus belongs both to Christology and to Jewish martyrdom. Through this line of thought, a new and mostly unperceived dimension accrues to the sorrowful Mary. As we will further clarify, the real Mary is a symbol for the church as well as for the Jewish community into which she was born and of which she had been a part. From a purely human point of view, Mary is a suffering Jewish mother. It ennobles rather than profanes her memory if the many Jewish mothers who have similarly experienced suffering recognize her simply and concretely as a worried and suffering Jewish mother.

One should not simply dismiss out of hand a Jew's ability to intuit feelingly how the Jewish mother Mary was concerned—and rightly so—as Jesus left her to devote himself to a dangerous way of life. And who is not deeply moved to read in John 19:26-27 concerning Jesus on the cross: "When Jesus saw his mother, and the disciple whom he loved standing near, he said to his mother, 'Woman, behold, your son!' Then he said to the disciple, 'Behold, your mother!' And from that hour the disciple took her to his home." Mary, the mother of Jesus, did not remain alone; she lived together with the apostles and the women (Acts 1:14). According to church tradition, she was also present at the miracle of Pentecost. This is an elevated destiny for a Jewish mother and it is good that the memory of this destiny is preserved in the Sacred Scripture of Christianity. If I have convinced only a few of my Christian readers of the Jewish paradigm in the life and suffering of Mary, it is an advance for the human understanding of the Jewish drama, which is temporally bound at the same time that it possesses transcendental worth.

I now come to the point I have occasionally mentioned. As many know, the Passion of Jesus has in the course of time frequently led to a not entirely appropriate tension with his Jewish brothers in the flesh. Among others, the Second Vatican Council has articulated the danger of anti-Semitism in relation to the Passion of Jesus. I personally can understand that the crucifixion, which was carried out by the Romans, could lead to a distorted understanding and a tension with Judaism. But it is especially remarkable that this tension could find expression in a medieval accusation placed in the mouth of the sorrowful mother of Jesus under the cross. How is it possible to have read such a thing into this grief of the mother? But this is exactly what happened in the amazing Latin accusation of Mary. It was written by Gottfried of Saint Victor (d. c. 1194). It can be found in the bilingual edition of the *Carmina Burana* (Munich, 1974), 736–43.

8

This splendid poem belongs among the highpoints of the Latin hymnody of the Middle Ages. It begins with the words "*Planctus ante nescia*" ("Complaint was unknown to me"). According to this poem, Mary blames the envious Jewish people for causing the death of Jesus. Their wild "conservatives" nailed him to the cross.

> What crime, what indignity
> this harsh people has perpetrated
> chains, whip, wounds
> nails, thorns, a cross's death
> he acquired with no fault.

And Mary prophesies to her own people, the Jews:

> Hunger, death blow, every need
> you experience yet what it means
> that you saw your Jesus dead
> and Barabbas living on.

Many a Christian will not even notice that this is a threatening and aggressive attitude against an entire group of human beings. After being heard for generations, these tones have become familiar. And I personally do not wish to contribute to the evil in the world by an aggressive critique of this attitude. But I would like to mention one thing in all of this that does not please me, namely, that such a verse was placed in the mouth of a sorrowful and accusing Mary under the cross. According to the following verses, there is a way out for the Jews—the baptism that is offered to them:

> People, so blind, so wretched
> be tutored in penance and contrition

even now avail yourselves
of the grace of Jesus newly given you.

Many of my Christian readers would approve of this sentiment. However, no more about that! According to a medieval legend, Mary herself had dictated this lamentation to a monk because only she could adequately express her grievances.

We want, however, to pick up on the more human, warm tones of the Christian devotion to Mary. We do not need depth psychology in order to comprehend this devotion but need only an understanding human heart. Because of Christian belief in Jesus, his mother was elevated to the sphere of holiness. She became, so to speak, the vessel of holiness. For the believing Christian, Jesus is divine and his holiness is supernatural. For that reason, the mother of Jesus in being fully human is much more accessible and comprehensible to a Christian who is stunned by the holiness. And because she was elevated to the sphere of holiness, Mary also became for the believing Christian a paradigm and exemplar of what Christians could become. The more Mary was understood to be human, the more she became a model for them. The belief in her virginity need not lead to an unnatural asceticism but can protect the believer from unchasteness and lead toward a spotless and shining purity.

Mary became simultaneously symbolic of the pure mother and through devotion to her one can understand and preserve the divine element in the birth of every child. If the devotion to Mary is supposed to contribute to the betterment of humanity, then one should also understand her sorrow for her dead, murdered, and faultless Son in terms of his being a model for and representative of all human suffering, and especially for a mother's pain.

And, as a Jew, I cannot avoid seeing Mary as the sorrowful, Jewish mother whose guiltless Son became the sacrifice of hatred for Jews. Especially today, after the incomprehensibility of the Holocaust, this aspect of the so-called Mariology could heal many wounds and lead to a more sympathetic attitude toward the people who are of the same race as Mary. We pray that the faithful Christian devotion to Mary might bear such fruit.

Mary, the woman and mother who actually lived, has been understood as a symbol for the church since the time of the church fathers. In the Old as well as the New Testament there are symbolic feminine figures who are supposed to embody a community, a people. As early as the Old Testament prophets, we see Israel presented in the symbol of a woman. What John on the island of Patmos reports to us in the twelfth chapter of his Revelation is especially important for the visionary, allegorical symbol of Mary as church. There the seer speaks: "And a great portent appeared in heaven, a woman clothed with the sun, with the moon under her feet, and on her head a crown of twelve stars; she was with child and she cried out in pangs of birth, in anguish for delivery." The woman is pursued by the devil in the form of a dragon and she gives birth to a son. We can't relate here the entire content of the sublime vision. A lot has been written on it and since the time of the church fathers it has been variously interpreted. More than once parallels that have been drawn from the Essene book of hymns from Qumran have clarified the mysteries of the vision.

But one thing was clear: the son to whom the woman gave birth is the Messiah. For that reason, the pregnant woman was seen to be a cosmic symbol for Mary, and the vision in the twelfth chapter of the Revelation of John is reflected in many Marian images. At the same time, it is without doubt that the woman in the revelation is a symbol for the community of the faithful and of the martyrs—for the church. On this basis the connection was developed between Mary and her importance as symbol for the church. And I presume that other explanations of Mary in terms of the holy community of the faithful have been a consequence of the vision in the twelfth chapter of the Revelation of John.

The attempt has often been made to uncover the prehistory of the vision of the pregnant woman in Revelation. It has often been ventured that the woman had originally been a feminine symbolic figure for the people Israel, who in messianic labor gave birth to the Messiah. In my opinion, this surmise is not beside the point. Could it possibly be that in the representation of the woman on Patmos, John had in mind the community of the Christian faithful and at the same time the holy community of Israel? That would not be a misrepresentation of the ecclesial vision of the composer of Revelation. It is difficult to determine to what extent he had thought of Mary in the vision of the pregnant woman who gave birth to the Messiah. But the thought of the historical mother of Jesus asserts itself. In any case, Christian theologians and thinkers were justified in interpreting the woman of the twelfth chapter of Revelation as Mary.

It is a shame that this is not the place to meditate further on this exciting material. We have reached one conclusion: on the level of symbol, we were able to discover a connection between Mary, the church, and the people Israel. That opens new horizons that will perhaps prove to be fruitful. But we should not ascend into the rarefied air of symbolism in order to discover in Mary that which is exemplarily Jewish. As we have already seen, it is incontestable that, historically speaking, Mary is the certain link between Jesus and the Jewish people. The Savior of the Christian faith was born of a Jewish woman named Mary. The Romans crucified him as king of the Jews. I hope that it will be properly understood when I say that, humanly speaking, Jesus was one among countless Jewish men who traveled the road of death to martyrdom. That is unfortunately especially clear in our day. For that reason, Mary also belongs to the countless Jewish mothers who lament their cruelly murdered Jewish children. I personally know such Jewish mothers who exist here and now and are not some abstraction. They have lost their children in the great mass murder in Europe. But there are also those who here in the land of Mary lament their children in appeasable pain—their sons who here and now have lost their lives because of a blind hatred of Jews. As I see it, it would not be such a bad Mariology that did not forget these sisters of Mary in the flesh.

The Jewish aspect of the figure of Mary is outlined both by her Jewish descent and by her typically Jewish fate. But we also by no means wish to lose sight of the universal human validity of Mary. In the Christian faith she was exalted among women in order that she might in turn exalt all women, and especially mothers. Through her sufferings, human suffering is made holy. If this is the direction in which Mary is valued, then this feeling crosses over all confessional boundaries. Then the remembrance of the pure mother of Jesus can at least in some way remove the defilement of modern humanity.

The Life of Mary

Pictorial Gallery

For the art of both the West and the East the figure of Mary, the God-bearer, is a theme of special importance. From the first depiction of Mary, which is attributed to the evangelist Luke—for which reason the various artist fraternities and guilds chose him as their patron—up to the present time, tens of thousands of images of Mary have been created in all areas of the plastic arts. Next to the individual depictions of the mother Mary with the child Jesus, the cyclical series of images that depict the life of Mary and her son were especially popular with the painters and sculptors since the Middle Ages, and they also expressed the wishes of those who commissioned the works. It is true that the evangelists say very little about the life of Mary. But the artists found rich stimulation for the development of themes in the New Testament apocryphal writings, the *Protogospel of James*, the *Gospel of Pseudo-Matthew*, and, above all, in the collection *Legenda Aurea* of the Dominican Jacobus de Voragine (1228–98).

The image sequence of these volumes portrays a life of Mary that is depicted especially in the scenes of two altars from the period of German Gothic—the Buxtehuder Altar from the workshop of Meister Bertram (c. 1410, Kunsthalle, Hamburg) and the Altar of the Master of the Golden Panel at Lüneburg (c. 1418, Niedersächsische Landesmuseum, Hannover). In the joyfulness of narration, which transforms each one of these paintings into a means of devotion and meditation, the brilliantly colorful depictions give witness to the great veneration in which the simple folk especially held the figure of the mother of God. This interest in Mary since the times of the ancient church also explains the blossoming creation of legends that communicated to the faithful something more and always something new about Mary.

The Background, Birth, and Childhood of Mary

plate 1 *The refusal of the Sacrifice of Joachim.* Panel of the Buxtehuder Altar.

As all the people went forth to sacrifice to the Lord, Joachim, a rich man in Israel who was always extremely generous in his offerings to the Lord, was turned back by the priest Ruben with the words, "It is not proper for you to bring your offering, for you have not begotten any offspring in Israel."

plate 2 *The Desert of Judah.*

Joachim turned away in sorrow and went into the desert and fasted forty days and forty nights. He said to himself, "I will not go back down until the Lord my God has visited me. Prayer will be my food and my drink."

At the same time in the house of Joachim, his wife, Anna, bemoaned being without child.

plate 3 *The Message of the Angel to Joachim.* Panel of the Buxtehuder Altar.

While Anna was in her garden, the angel of the Lord approached her and said, "You will conceive and bear a child." And two messengers came to her and said, "Joachim, your husband, is coming with his flocks, for an angel announced to him: 'Go down! Behold, Anna, your wife, will conceive in her body!'"

plate 4 *Joachim and Anna Meet at the Door.* Panel of the Buxtehuder Altar.

As Joachim came with his flocks, Anna stood at the door. She saw Joachim coming and she ran to him and threw her arms around his neck and said, "Now I know that God the Lord has richly blessed you. For behold, I, who was childless, will conceive." On this day Joachim rested in his house.

plate 5 *The Birth of Mary.* Panel of the Buxtehuder Altar.

In the ninth month Anna bore her child. And she said to the midwife, "To what have I given birth?" The midwife answered, "A little girl." And Anna cried out, "On this day is my spirit exalted." After the birth of the child, Anna purified herself, nursed the child at her breast, and gave her the name Mary.

plate 6 *The Education of Mary by Her Mother, Anna.* Portion of an East English altar (1325–39). Musée Cluny, Paris.

Even though the apocryphal gospels relate stories of Mary's growing up, her early maturity, and her extraordinary abilities, there is no mention of the instruction of the child by her mother. This scene is rare for this period, and such depictions appear more frequently with the growing veneration of Anna in the fifteenth century.

plate 7 *Mary and Christ as the Most Important Shoots of the "Root of Jesse."* Miniature.

There are many allusions supporting this pictorial theme in both the Old and the New Testaments. We recall here the hymn "Lo, how a rose e'er blooming / From tender stem hath sprung!"

Mary as a Temple Virgin, the Betrothal, the Beginning of Her Motherhood

plate 8 *The Steps of the Temple in Jerusalem.*

plate 9 *The High Priest Receives Mary as a Temple Virgin.* Panel of the Monks' Altar in Göttingen.

plate 10 *Mary, the Temple Virgin, in Prayer.* Upper Rhine panel painting (c. 1445). Frauenhausmuseum, Strasbourg.

Joachim and Anna decided to consecrate their daughter Mary to the Lord and to bring her to the temple. When the child was three years old, they brought her up to the temple, but they feared that she might not remain there. The priest received her, kissed her, and blessed her with the words, "The Lord has made your name great among all generations. At the end of days, the Lord will reveal in you his salvation for the sons of Israel!" He placed her on the third step of the altar, and God the Lord filled the child with gracefulness and her little feet danced for joy and she was the delight of the whole house of Israel. Her parents went down from the temple. They were amazed and filled with thanks and praise for God the Almighty because the child had not turned back to them. But Mary remained sheltered like a dove in the temple and received nourishment from the hand of an angel.

When she was twelve years old, there was a consultation of priests, who said, "Behold, Mary has become twelve years old in the temple of the Lord. What should we do with her so that she does not stain the temple of the Lord?" And they said to the high priest, "You stand at the altar of the Lord. Go into the Holy of Holies and pray for her. We want to do whatever the Lord reveals to you." And the high priest took the amulet with the twelve small bells and went into the Holy of Holies and prayed for her. And behold, an angel of the Lord stood suddenly before him and spoke to him, "Zachariah, Zachariah, go out and gather together the widowers of the people (each of them is supposed to carry a staff) and she is to be the wife of the one to whom the Lord gives a miraculous sign!" (According to the *Protogospel of James*)

plate 11 *The High Priest Betrothes Mary to Joseph.* Panel of the Monks' Altar in Göttingen.

After the men had gathered together, the high priest collected their staffs and went with these into the temple to pray. He returned from the temple and gave back the staffs to the men. No miraculous sign appeared on these. Joseph received the last staff, and, behold, a dove came forth from the staff and flew onto the head of Joseph. Then the priest spoke to Joseph, "Joseph, it falls to you to receive the virgin of the Lord. Take her into your care!" But Joseph answered him, "I already have sons and am old, but she is a young girl. I fear I will become the laughingstock of the sons of Israel." Then the priest spoke to Joseph: "Fear the Lord your God and think on all that God did to Dathan, Abiram, and Korah, how the earth opened up and they because of their stubbornness were all devoured. Be concerned now, Joseph, that this does not also occur in your house!" And Joseph was afraid and took her into his care. And Joseph said to her, "Mary, I have received you out of the temple of the Lord and I take you now into my house. I am going forth to set up my barns. Afterwards, I will come back to you. The Lord will protect you!" (According to the *Protogospel of James*)

plate 12 *The Annunciation*. Panel of the Buxtehuder Altar.

In the sixth month the angel Gabriel was sent from God to a city of Galilee named Nazareth, to a virgin betrothed to a man whose name was Joseph, of the house of David; and the virgin's name was Mary. And he came to her and said, "Hail, O favored one, the Lord is with you." But she was greatly troubled at the saying, and considered in her mind what sort of greeting this might be. And the angel said to her, "Do not be afraid, Mary, for you have found favor with God. And behold, you will conceive in your womb and bear a son, and you shall call his name Jesus. He will be great, and will be called the Son of the Most High; and the Lord God will give to him the throne of his father David, and he will reign over the house of Jacob for ever; and of his kingdom there will be no end."

And Mary said to the angel, "How shall this be, since I have no husband?" And the angel said to her, "The Holy Spirit will come upon you, and the power of the Most High will overshadow you; therefore the child to be born will be called holy, the Son of God. And behold, your kinswoman Elizabeth in her old age has also conceived a son; and this is the sixth month with her who was called barren. For with God nothing will be impossible." And Mary said, "Behold, I am the handmaid of the Lord; let it be to me according to your word." And the angel departed from her. (Luke 1:26-38)

plate 13 *View of the Area of Ain Karim, the Home of Elizabeth.*

plate 14 *The Visitation*. Panel of the Buxtehuder Altar.

In those days Mary arose and went with haste into the hill country, to a city of Judah, and she entered the house of Zechariah and greeted Elizabeth. And when Elizabeth heard the greeting of Mary, the babe leaped in her womb; and Elizabeth was filled with the Holy Spirit and she exclaimed with a loud cry, "Blessed are you among women, and blessed is the fruit of your womb! . . ." And Mary said, "My soul magnifies the Lord, and my spirit rejoices in God my Savior, for he has regarded the low estate of his handmaiden. For behold, henceforth all generations will call me blessed; for he who is mighty has done great things for me, and holy is his name." (Luke 1:39-42, 46-49)

plate 15 *The Hopeful Mary.* Picture from the panel (c. 1420) of the Marian Altar of the Strasbourg Cathedral. Frauenhausmuseum, Strasbourg.

When she was in her sixth month, behold, Joseph came from his building and, as he entered the house, he found her pregnant. And he slapped his face, threw himself on the bed, cried bitterly, and spoke: "How am I to face the Lord my God? For I received you from the temple of the Lord as a virgin and have not protected you. Who is the one who has deceived me?" And behold, an angel of the Lord appeared to him in a dream and spoke: "Do not be afraid on account of this maiden. For that which is in her comes from the Holy Spirit. She will bear a son, and you are to give him the name Jesus, for he will save his people from their sins." And Joseph got up from his sleep, praised the God of Israel, who had been gracious to him, and he took her from then on into his care. (According to the *Protogospel of James*)

The Birth of the Lord

plate 16 *The Region of Bethlehem.*

plate 17 *The Birth of Jesus.* Panel of the Buxtehuder Altar.

In those days a decree went out from Caesar Augustus that all the world should be enrolled. This was the first enrollment, when Quirinius was governor of Syria. And all went to be enrolled, each to his own city. And Joseph also went up from Galilee, from the city of Nazareth, to Judea, to the city of David, which is called Bethlehem, because he was of the house and lineage of David, to be enrolled with Mary, his betrothed, who was with child. And while they were there, the time came for her to be delivered. And she gave birth to her firstborn son and wrapped him in swaddling cloths, and laid him in a manger, because there was no room for them in the inn. (Luke 2:1-7)

plate 18 *The Announcing to the Shepherds.* Panel of the Buxtehuder Altar.

And in that region there were shepherds out in the field, keeping watch over their flock by night. And an angel of the Lord appeared to them, and the glory of the Lord shone around them, and they were filled with fear. And the angel said to them, "Be not afraid; for behold, I bring you good news of a great joy which will come to all the people; for to you is born this day in the city of David a Savior, who is Christ the Lord. And this will be a sign for you: you will find a babe wrapped in swaddling cloths and lying in a manger." And suddenly there was with the angel a multitude of the heavenly host praising God and saying, "Glory to God in the highest, and on earth peace among men with whom he is pleased!" (Luke 2:8-14)

plate 19 *The Circumcision of the Lord.* Panel of the Buxtehuder Altar.

And at the end of eight days, when he was circumcised, he was called Jesus, the name given him by the angel before he was conceived in the womb. (Luke 2:21)

plate 20 *The Adoration of the Magi from the East.* Panel of the Buxtehuder Altar.

Now when Jesus was born in Bethlehem of Judea in the days of Herod the king, behold, wise men from the East came to Jerusalem, saying, "Where is he who has been born king of the Jews? For we have seen his star in the East, and have come to worship him." When Herod the king heard this, he was troubled, and all Jerusalem with him.

Then Herod summoned the wise men secretly and ascertained from them what time the star appeared; and he sent them to Bethlehem, saying, "Go and search diligently for the child, and when you have found him bring me word, that I too may come and worship him." When they had heard the king they went their way; and lo, the star which they had seen in the East went before them, till it came to rest over the place where the child was. When they saw the star, they rejoiced exceedingly with great joy; and going into the house they saw the child with Mary his mother, and they fell down and worshiped him. Then, opening their treasures, they offered him gifts, gold and frankincense and myrrh. (Matt. 2:1-3, 7-11)

plate 21 *The Presentation of Jesus in the Temple.* Panel of the Buxtehuder Altar.

And when the time came for their purification according to the law of Moses, they brought him up to Jerusalem to present him to the Lord (as it is written in the law of the Lord, "Every male that opens the womb shall be called holy to the Lord") and to offer a sacrifice according to what is said in the law of the Lord, "a pair of turtledoves, or two young pigeons." Now there was a man in Jerusalem, whose name was Simeon, and this man was righteous and devout, looking for the consolation of Israel, and the Holy Spirit was upon him. And it had been revealed to him by the Holy Spirit that he would not see death before he had seen the Lord's Christ. And inspired by the Spirit he came into the temple; and when the parents brought in the child Jesus, to do for him according to the custom of the law, he took him up in his arms and blessed God and said, "Lord, now lettest thou thy servant depart in peace, according to thy word; for mine eyes have seen thy salvation which thou hast prepared in the presence of all peoples, a light for revelation to the Gentiles, and for glory to thy people Israel." And his father and mother marveled at what was said about him; and Simeon blessed them and said to Mary his mother, "Behold, this child is set for the fall and rising of many in Israel, and for a sign that is spoken against (and a sword will pierce through your own soul also), that thoughts out of many hearts may be revealed."

And there was a prophetess, Anna, the daughter of Phanuel, of the tribe of Asher; she was of a great age, having lived with her husband seven years from her virginity. . . . And coming up at that very hour she gave thanks to God, and spoke of him to all who were looking for the redemption of Jerusalem. (Luke 2:22-36, 38)

plate 22 *Herod Orders the Massacre of the Children of Bethlehem.* Panel of the Buxtehuder Altar.
Then Herod, when he saw he had been tricked by the wise men, was in a furious rage, and he sent and killed all the male children in Bethlehem and in all that region who were two years old or under, according to the time which he had ascertained from the wise men. (Matt. 2:16)

plate 23 *The Flight into Egypt.* Panel of the Buxtehuder Altar.
Now when [the wise men] had departed, behold, an angel of the Lord appeared to Joseph in a dream and said, "Rise, take the child and his mother, and flee to Egypt, and remain there till I tell you; for Herod is about to search for the child, to destroy him." And he rose and took the child and his mother by night, and departed to Egypt, and remained there until the death of Herod. This was to fulfill what the Lord has spoken by the prophet, "Out of Egypt have I called my son." (Matt. 2:13-15)

The Childhood of Jesus

plate 24 *Mary with Her Son.* Panel painting by Gentile da Fabriano (c. 1410). Museo Nazionale, Pisa.

20

plate 25 *View of Nazareth.*

But when Herod died, behold, an angel of the Lord appeared in a dream to Joseph in Egypt, saying, "Rise, take the child and his mother, and go to the land of Israel, for those who sought the child's life are dead." And he rose and took the child and his mother, and went to the land of Israel. But when he heard that Archelaus reigned over Judea in place of his father Herod, he was afraid to go there, and being warned in a dream he withdrew to the district of Galilee. And he went and dwelt in a city called Nazareth, that what was spoken by the prophets might be fulfilled, "He shall be called a Nazarene." (Matt. 2:19-23)

plate 26 *Visit of the Angel in Nazareth.* Panel of the Buxtehuder Altar.

One day as the child Jesus was with his parents, two angels appeared to him and his mother. They carried the cross, the nails, the crown of thorns, and the lance—the instruments of his Passion—with which the Lord would someday be tortured and killed. This was the first announcement of the Passion of the Lord. (According to the *Legenda Aurea*)

plate 27 *View of the Sea of Galilee.*

Joseph lived with Jesus and his mother in the city of Nazareth in Galilee. And the child grew and became strong, filled with wisdom; and the favor of God was upon him.

plate 28 *The return from Egypt to Nazareth.* Mosaic in Hora Church, Istanbul.

Joseph carries the infant Jesus on his shoulders, Mary follows, a youth leads the donkey.

plate 29 *The Old Roman Road toward Jerusalem.*

plate 30 *Jesus among the Teachers.* Panel of the Buxtehuder Altar.

Now his parents went to Jerusalem every year at the feast of the Passover. And when he was twelve years old, they went up according to custom; and when the feast was ended, as they were returning, the boy Jesus stayed behind in Jerusalem. His parents did not know it, but supposing him to be in the company they went a day's journey, and they sought him among their kinsfolk and acquaintances; and when they did not find him, they returned to Jerusalem, seeking him.

After three days they found him in the temple, sitting among the teachers, listening to them and asking them questions; and all who heard him were amazed at his understanding and his answers. And when they saw him they were astonished; and his mother said to him, "Son, why have you treated us so? Behold, your father and I have been looking for you anxiously." And he said to them, "How is it that you sought me? Did you not know that I must be in my Father's house?" And they did not understand the saying which he spoke to them. (Luke 2:41-50)

From the Wedding in Cana to the Resurrection

plate 31 *View of the Sea of Galilee.*
Now when he heard that John had been arrested, he withdrew into Galilee; and leaving Nazareth he went and dwelt in Capernaum by the sea, in the territory of Zebulun and Naphtali, that what was spoken by the prophet Isaiah might be fulfilled: "The land of Zebulun and the land of Naphtali, toward the sea, across the Jordan, Galilee of the Gentiles—the people who sat in darkness have seen a great light, and for those who sat in the region and shadow of death light has dawned." From that time Jesus began to preach, saying, "Repent, for the kingdom of heaven is at hand." (Matt. 4:12-17)

plate 32 *River Jordan*, where Jesus was baptized by John the Baptist.

plate 33 *Jesus with Mary at the Wedding at Cana.* Panel of the Buxtehuder Altar.
On the third day there was a marriage at Cana in Galilee, and the mother of Jesus was there; Jesus also was invited to the marriage, with his disciples. When the wine gave out, the mother of Jesus said to him, "They have no wine." And Jesus said to her, "O woman, what have you to do with me? My hour has not yet come." His mother said to the servants, "Do whatever he tells you." Now six stone jars were standing there, for the Jewish rites of purification, each holding twenty or thirty gallons. Jesus said to them, "Fill the jars with water." And they filled them up to the brim. He said to them, "Now draw some out, and take it to the steward of the feast." So they took it. When the steward of the feast tasted the water now become wine, and did not know where it came from (though the servants who had drawn the water knew), the steward of the feast

called the bridegroom and said to him, "Every man serves the good wine first; and when men have drunk freely, then the poor wine; but you have kept the good wine until now." This, the first of his signs, Jesus did at Cana in Galilee, and manifested his glory; and his disciples believed in him.

After this he went down to Capernaum, with his mother and his brothers and his disciples; and there they stayed for a few days. (John 2:1-12)

plate 34 *Cana of Galilee.*

plate 35 *View toward Jerusalem from the Garden of the Mount of Olives.*
Now the Passover of the Jews was at hand, and many went up from the country to Jerusalem before the Passover, to purify themselves. They were looking for Jesus and saying to one another as they stood in the temple, "What do you think? That he will not come to the feast?" Now the chief priests and the Pharisees had given orders that if any one knew where he was, he should let them know, so that they might arrest him. (John 11:55-57)

plate 36 *Mount of Olives and Garden of Gethsemane across from Old City.*

plate 37 *Jesus Carries His Cross.* Panel from the Altar of the Master of the Golden Panel at Lüneburg.
And as they led him away, they seized one Simon of Cyrene, who was coming in from the country, and laid on him the cross, to carry it behind Jesus. And there followed him a great multitude of the people, and of women who bewailed and lamented him. But Jesus turning to them said, "Daughters of Jerusalem, do not weep for me, but weep for yourselves and for your children." (Luke 23:26-28)

plate 38 *Jesus on the Cross.* Panel from the Altar of the Master of the Golden Panel at Lüneburg.
And when they came to the place, which is called The Skull, there they crucified him, and the criminals, one on the right and one on the left. And the people stood by watching; but the rulers scoffed at him, saying, "He saved others; let him save himself, if he is the Christ of God, his Chosen One!" There was also an inscription over him, "This is the King of the Jews." (Luke 23:33, 35, 38)

Standing by the cross of Jesus were his mother, and his mother's sister, Mary the wife of Clopas, and Mary Magdalene. When Jesus saw his mother, and the disciple whom he loved standing near, he said to his mother, "Woman, behold, your son!" Then he said to the disciple, "Behold, your mother!" And from that hour the disciple took her to his own home. (John 19:25-27)

plate 39 *Jesus Is Taken Down from the Cross.* Panel from the Altar of the Master of the Golden Panel at Lüneburg.

plate 40 *Jesus Is Laid in the Tomb.* Panel from the Altar of the Master of the Golden Panel at Lüneburg.

It was now about the sixth hour, and there was darkness over the whole land until the ninth hour, while the sun's light failed; and the curtain of the temple was torn in two. Then Jesus, crying with a loud voice, said, "Father, into thy hands I commit my spirit!" And having said this he breathed his last. And all his acquaintances and the women who had followed him from Galilee stood at a distance and saw these things.

Now there was a man named Joseph from the Jewish town of Arimathea. He was a member of the council, a good and righteous man, who had not consented to their purpose and deed, and he was looking for the kingdom of God. This man went to Pilate and asked for the body of Jesus. Then he took it down and wrapped it in a linen shroud, and laid him in a rock-hewn tomb, where no one had ever yet been laid. It was the day of Preparation, and the Sabbath was beginning. The women who had come with him from Galilee followed, and saw the tomb, and how his body was laid. (Luke 23:44-46, 49-55)

plate 41 *The Women and the Angel at the Empty Tomb of Jesus.* Panel from the Altar of the Master of the Golden Panel at Lüneburg.

Now after the Sabbath, toward the dawn of the first day of the week, Mary Magdalene and the other Mary went to see the sepulcher. And behold, there was a great earthquake; for an angel of the Lord descended from heaven and came and rolled back the stone, and sat upon it. His appearance was like lightning, and his raiment white as snow. And for fear of him the guards trembled and became like dead men. But the angel said to the women, "Do not be afraid; for I know that you seek Jesus who was crucified. He is not here; for he has risen, as he said. Come, see the place where he lay. Then go quickly and tell his disciples that he has risen from the dead, and behold, he is going before you to Galilee; there you will see him. Lo, I have told you." So they departed quickly from the tomb with fear and great joy, and ran to tell his disciples. (Matt. 28:1-8)

From the Ascension of Christ
to the Crowning of Mary

plate 42 *The Ascension of Christ*. Panel from the Altar of the Master of the Golden Panel at Lüneburg.
Then he led them out as far as Bethany, and lifting up his hands he blessed them. While he blessed them, he parted from them, and was carried up into heaven. And they returned to Jerusalem with great joy, and were continually in the temple blessing God. (Luke 24:50-53)

plate 43 *The Upper Room in Jerusalem*.

plate 44 *The Descent of the Holy Spirit*. Panel from the Altar of the Master of the Golden Panel at Lüneburg.
Then they returned to Jerusalem from the mount called Olivet, which is near Jerusalem, a Sabbath day's journey away; and when they had entered, they went up to the upper room, where they were staying, Peter and John and James and Andrew, Philip and Thomas, Bartholomew and Matthew, James the son of Alphaeus and Simon the Zealot and Judas the son of James. All these with one accord devoted themselves to prayer, together with the women and Mary the mother of Jesus, and with his brothers.
When the day of Pentecost had come, they were all together in one place. And suddenly a sound came from heaven like the rush of a mighty wind, and it filled all the house where they were sitting. And there appeared to them tongues as of fire, distributed and resting on each one of them. And they were all filled with the Holy Spirit and began to speak in other tongues, as the Spirit gave them utterance. (Acts 1:12-14; 2:1-4)

plate 45 *Street in Ephesus with Houses from the First Century after Christ*.

plate 46 *The Death of Mary.* Panel from the Altar of the Master of the Golden Panel at Lüneburg.

Mary lived in a house on Mount Zion another twenty-four years after the death of her son—others say twelve years. As she reflected on this once again, an angel appeared and announced her death to her. But Mary wanted to see all the apostles around her once more. And so it happened: A white cloud brought John from Ephesus, where he preached. And similar things happened with all the apostles. As they were gathered around the dying Mary, Christ appeared and told his mother that he wanted to take her home. And just as she had been without stain in her life, Mary died without suffering and her soul flew into the arms of her son. (According to the *Legenda Aurea*)

plate 47 *The Assumption of Mary and the Giving of the Sash to Thomas.* Painting by Benozzo Gozzoli (c. 1450). Center panel of an altar. Vatican Museum, Rome.

The apostles buried the body of Mary as the Lord had commanded them and they remained for three days in prayer at her grave. Then Christ appeared to them. And the apostles said to him, "Lord, we think it right that you raise the body of your mother and set her at your right hand for all eternity." And the Lord had the archangel Michael summon the soul of Mary and he spoke: "Arise, my dove, you who are closest to me." Immediately the soul of Mary went into her body and she rose gloriously from the grave and she went up to heaven accompanied by a multitude of angels.

The apostle Thomas was not present at this event. When he arrived, he didn't believe the assumption of Mary. Suddenly a sash that Mary had worn dropped down from heaven so that Thomas could know that she had gone bodily up to heaven. (According to the *Legenda Aurea*)

plate 48 *The Crowning of Mary.* Panel of the Buxtehuder Altar.

Christ had already said to his dying mother, "Come to me, that you may be crowned." She had answered him, "Behold, I am coming, for it is written of me that I am to do your will, my God, and my spirit rejoices in you, the God of my salvation." (According to the *Legenda Aurea*)

plate 1

plate 2

plate 3

plate 4

plate 5

plate 6

plate 7

plate 8

plate 9

plate 10

plate 11

plate 12

plate 13

plate 14

plate 15

plate 16

plate 17

plate 18

plate 19

plate 20

plate 21

plate 22

plate 23

plate 24

plate 25

plate 26

plate 27

plate 28

plate 29

plate 30

plate 31

plate 32

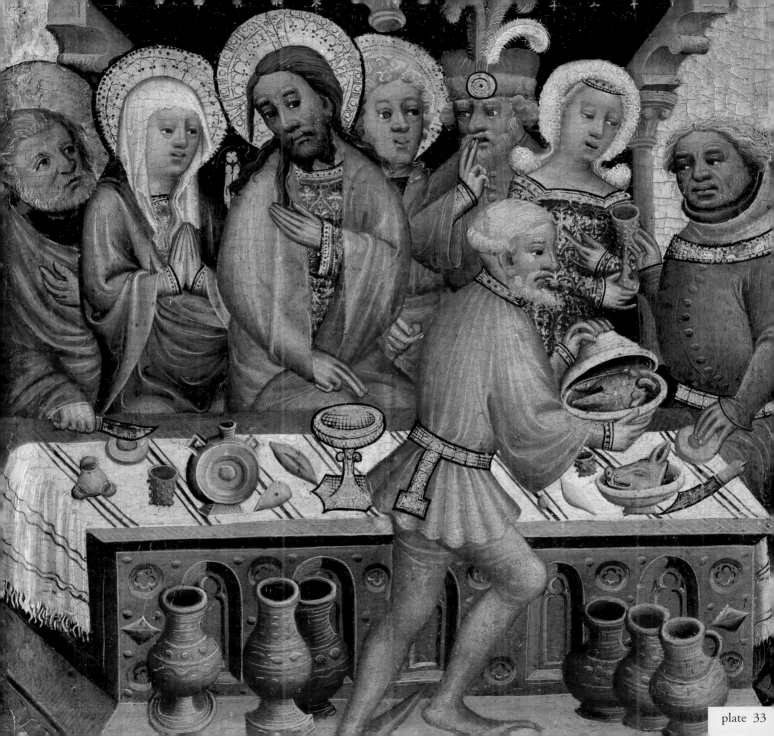

plate 33

plate 34

plate 35

plate 36

plate 37

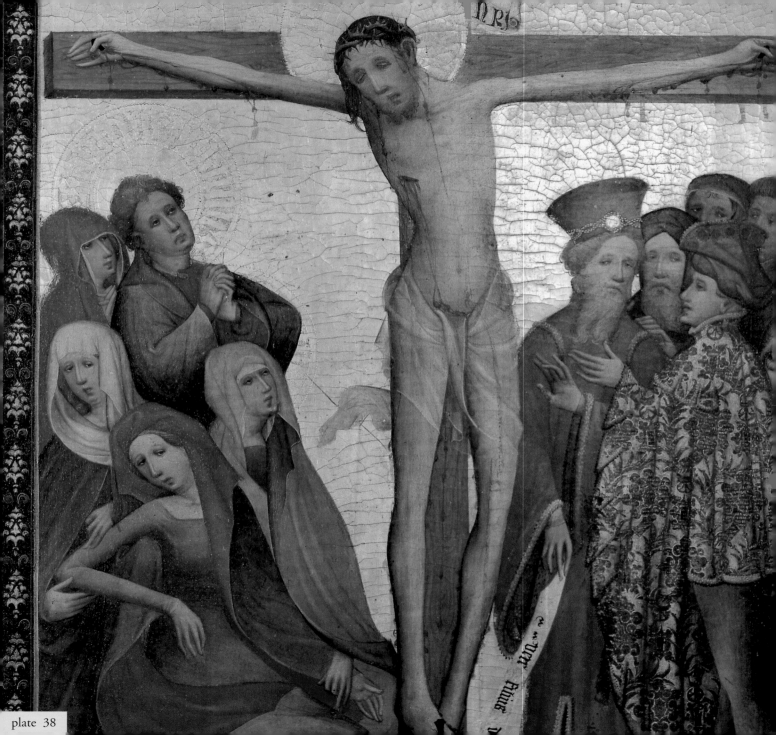

plate 38

plate 39

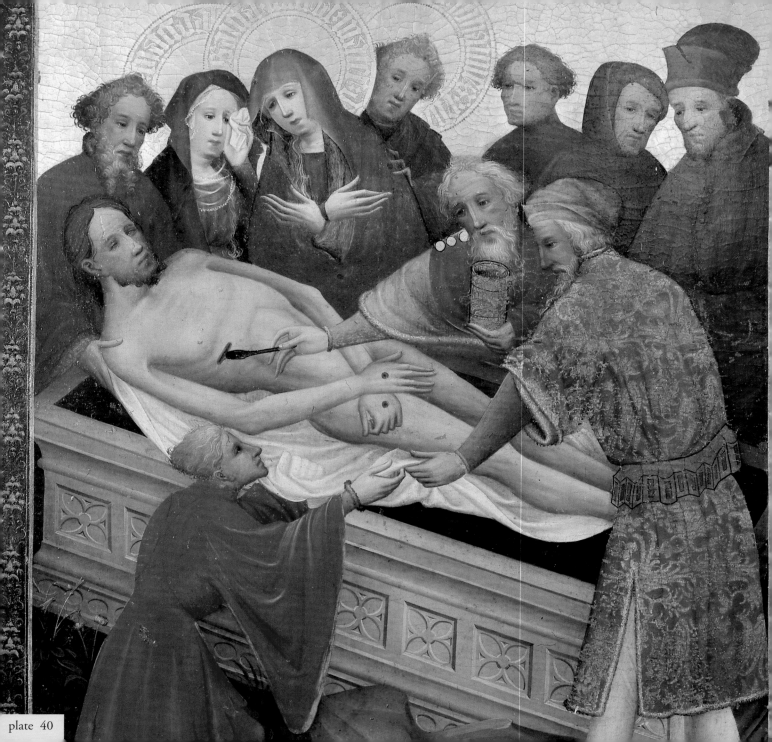

plate 40

Non est hic quem queritis surrexit sicut dixit

plate 41

plate 42

plate 43

plate 44

plate 45

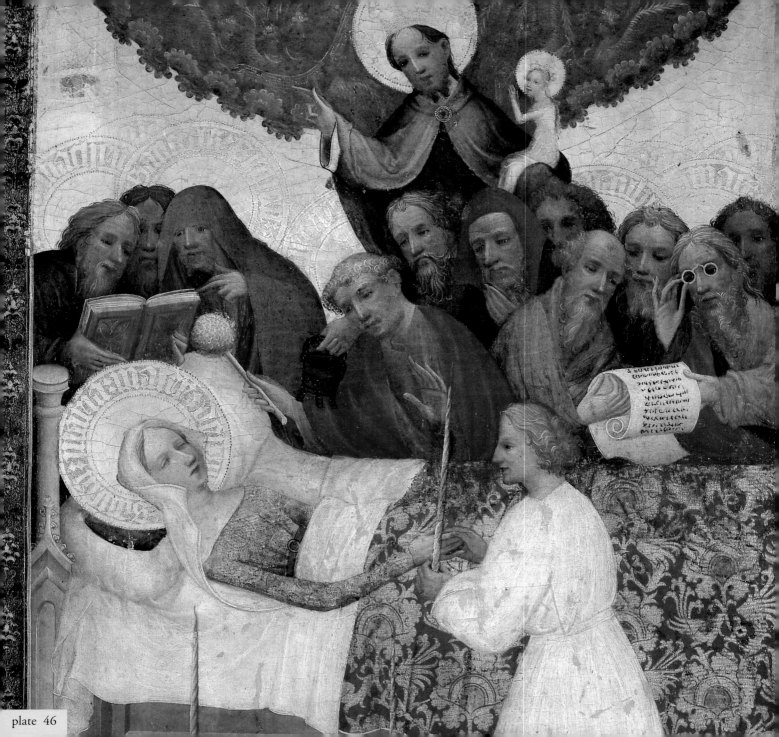

plate 46

plate 47

plate 48

Mary and Christian Doctrine

Jaroslav Pelikan

Quia respexit humilitatem ancillae suae:
Ecce enim ex hoc beatam me dicent omnes generationes.

These words of the virgin Mary from the Vulgate of Luke 1:48 are familiar to concertgoers, who have heard the settings of the Latin *Magnificat* by Roman Catholic composers from Palestrina to Penderecki—and, let it be remembered, by the stalwart Lutheran Johann Sebastian Bach as well: "For behold, henceforth all generations will call me blessed." But are the words true? Have all generations indeed called her blessed? Or is the neglect of devotion to her in the Protestant churches and the absence of doctrine about her simply proof of how human and fallible she really was?

The answers to those questions lie above all in a clarification of the development of the doctrine of Mary. "I consider," wrote the late American Jesuit theologian John Courtney Murray, "that the parting of the ways between the two Christian communities [Roman Catholic and Protestant] takes place on the issue of the development of doctrine." And then, with characteristic sharpness, he put that issue: "I do not think that the first ecumenical question is, what think ye of the Church? Or even, what think ye of Christ? The dialogue would rise out of the current confusion if the first question raised were, what think ye of the Nicene homoousion?" By this Father Murray meant to suggest that the homoousion formula adopted by the Council of Nicaea in 325, which most of Protestantism also accepts, legitimates a development of Christian doctrine beyond the language and thought-world of the New Testament. And if such development was legitimate, where finally are the limits of legitimacy?

Nevertheless, as the late German Jesuit theologian Karl Rahner pointed out in an essay with the significant title (and with significant quotation marks in the title) "The 'New' Dogma," published in 1950 as a commentary on the promulgation of the dogma of the Assumption of the Virgin, the doctrine of Mary is in many ways the most striking among all the examples of "doctrinal development," *Dogmenentwicklung*—a phenomenon to which Father Rahner would often return, not only in his book of 1956, *Mary the Mother of the Lord*, but in many articles on the relation between dogma and its history. For even the most inclusive method of reading the New Testament must acknowledge that the explicit, *ex professo*, references to Mary in its pages are both few in number and brief in scope: it would probably be possible to print all of them on a few pages of this book. Yet the pages of this book and above all the sumptuous plates in this book are evidence of the "development" both of doctrine and of devotion. It is significant that a consideration of the place of Mary in the plan of God has repeatedly served in the history of the doctrine of Jesus Christ himself as an epitome of the church's confession about him: Christology and Mariology are inextricable but in both directions. It is no less significant, however, that Christian communions and theologians differ from one another in their interpretation of Mary principally on the basis of where they set the terminus ad quem, the final point, for the development. It is an index of the centrality of the understanding of the development of doctrine for the doctrine of Mary, therefore, that a review of the history of this development is at the same time an ecumenical cartography of the present state of doctrine and devotion.

Authentication of the True Humanity of Jesus

The oldest phrase of the New Testament to refer to Mary appears in the Epistle to the Galatians (4:4), where the Son of God is said to have been "born of [a] woman," *genomenon ek gynaikos*. This is, as a recent volume, *Mary in the New Testament*, puts it, "a frequently-used Jewish expression to designate a person's human condition"; and as Shakespeare's Macbeth shows, "one of woman born" has continued in various modern languages to identify someone as genuinely human—no less than human but not necessarily more than human.

Because the earliest christological heresy appears to have been Docetism, the denial of the true humanity of Jesus, the earliest Mariological heresy may be said to have been the same: Jesus had passed through the body of Mary as light passes through a window, some early heretics suggested, and therefore he only seemed to have a human body. To such suggestions the champions of orthodoxy replied that since the heretics "were apprehensive that the belief in a fleshly body would also entail the belief in a birth, undoubtedly he who seemed to be human was believed to have been really and truly born" (Tertullian). A true birth from a true mother was the authentication of his true humanity. Hence it was not the canonical Gospels of Matthew and Luke, the only two that contain a Nativity story, but apocryphal gospels of dubious provenance, that professed to find anything unusual in the birth itself, as distinct from the conception. It was as though the church, before allowing itself to engage in high-flown speculations about the special circumstances of Jesus' birth or the special privileges of his mother, needed first to nail down tight the fully human character of the birth and of the Child.

It seems unwarranted to read anything further into the phrase from Galatians, as though "born of a woman" necessarily implied "but not of a man and a woman." Thus the phrase made Mary the authentication of the true humanity of Jesus. For the ancient world, as the myths of gods and heroes suggest, one human parent was necessary to assure that a person was genuinely human, and one of the roles assigned to Mary from the beginning has been that of providing this assurance. Some scholars have even maintained that the primary force of the phrase "born of the virgin Mary" in the Apostles' Creed was to express this same insistence of the church upon the authentic humanity of the man Jesus.

That insistence has been the irreducible minimum in all the theories about Mary that have appeared in the history of orthodox Christianity, and it underlies the artistic representations (as in plates 5 and 7) of her own birth and childhood. Indeed, those who in modern times have denied the virginal conception of Jesus and hence the virginity of his mother have usually claimed to be doing so in the name of this same insistence upon authentic humanity. Except for such heretics as the Docetists, therefore, everyone has agreed that Jesus was "born of a woman." The disagreement has come over where it was necessary, or permissible, to say more than that, and how much more.

From plate 12 depicting the Annunciation (or, as it is known in Greek, the *euangelismos*), it is evident that a corollary of the phrase "born of a woman" was her free assent to that role, as expressed in the words of Luke 1:38: *Ecce ancilla Domini, fit mihi secundum, verbum tuum* ("Behold, I am the handmaid of the Lord; let it be to me according to your word"). For while she was seen as *gratia plena* (full of grace), as the angelic salutation on plate 12 indicates, that divine grace was not to be interpreted as having overwhelmed her at the cost of her free will and thus of her own authentic humanity. This is the original basis for the title of coredemptrix that eventually came to be assigned to Mary in Roman Catholic theology. Her participation in the redemption was granted freely because she was the exemplar of how human free will and divine grace act together as well.

Repeatedly in the history of Christian devotion and Christian art and literature, it has become necessary to reassert the true humanity of the Mother as well as of the Son. Plate 38, representing Mary at the foot of the cross, and the Pietà in plate 39, representing her with the dead body of her Son, have their literary and musical counterpart in the many *Marienklagen* that became so popular in the later Middle Ages and since. One of the most beloved nonliturgical hymns from the medieval period has been set to music by countless composers, including Palestrina, Rossini, and Dvořák, and translated into many languages, with perhaps as many as one hundred German versions alone:

Stabat Mater dolorosa	At the cross, her station keeping.
juxta Crucem lacrimosa,	Stood the mournful mother weeping,
dum pendebat Filius;	Close to Jesus to the last:
cujus animam gementem	Through her heart, his sorrow sharing,
contristantem et dolentem	All his bitter anguish bearing,
pertransivit gladius.	Now at length the sword had passed.

Virgin Mother

By far the most voluminous narratives about Mary in the New Testament are the infancy stories in the Gospels of Matthew and Luke. They are directly or indirectly also the principal source for almost half the anecdotes presented here in the plates. The repetition of the statement that Mary "kept these things in her heart" (Luke 2:19, 51), when related to the reference, in the prolegomena of the Gospel, to the author's research based on the testimony of "eyewitnesses" (Luke 1:1-4), led various interpreters to regard the infancy narratives of the Third Gospel as the memoirs of the virgin Mary herself. The decidedly Hebraic cast of the language in those two chapters and especially in their canticles (the *Magnificat, Benedictus,* and *Nunc Dimittis*) was taken as further substantiation of this interpretation, which, if accepted, would affect the credibility of their narrative, including perhaps the narrative of the conception as such. But few if any New Testament scholars today take this theory about the sources of Luke's Gospel very seriously.

Luke does explicitly clarify his version of the genealogy of Jesus by stating that he was "the son (as was supposed) of Joseph" (Luke 3:23). In the Gospel of Matthew, on the other hand, the genealogy is less clear. The generally accepted text of Matthew 1:16 refers to "Joseph the husband of Mary, of whom [*ex hēs*, namely, of Mary] Jesus was born, who is called Christ." But there are many variants in the manuscripts and versions; none of them may lay claim to contesting seriously the validity of the accepted reading, but taken together they are evidence for the ambiguity of the question in some early

Christian circles. One version of the verse even reads, "Joseph begat Jesus, who is called Christ."

Whatever the status of the sources or manuscripts and versions may be, the infancy narratives in Matthew and Luke, whether or not they were added or amended later, now stand as integral parts of the two books. In their present form, both accounts make a point of asserting that Jesus was conceived in the womb of Mary without a human father. Matthew has Joseph resolving "to divorce her quietly" when "she was found to be with child of the Holy Spirit," but being deterred by a vision in a dream (Matt. 1:18-25); Luke has Mary ask the angel of the Annunciation, "How shall this be, since I have no husband?" and being told by the angel that "the Holy Spirit will come upon you, and the power of the Most High will overshadow you" (Luke 1:34-35). Mary was, accordingly and miraculously, both a virgin and a mother. As Bernard of Clairvaux would put it, her uniqueness was to be found in her having been both of these at the same time.

The miracle of her virginity early became the object of both wonder and speculation (see below). On the basis of the narratives in Matthew and Luke, it was the unanimous teaching of all the orthodox fathers of the church, eastern and western, amounting to what one student of patristic Mariology has called a patristic consensus, that Mary conceived her Son with her virginity unimpaired. This teaching was enshrined in the phrase of the Apostles' Creed "born of the virgin Mary." In their expositions of the Creed, Luther, Calvin, and Bullinger affirmed it, together with other "privileges" of Mary, including some of the postbiblical ones, as a recent compilation of their praises for Mary (*Marienlob der Reformatoren*) has amply documented. In this own exposition of the *Magnificat*, Luther affirmed the miracle of Mary's virginity but joined himself to the medieval tradition by declaring that her faith in the Word of God was an even greater miracle.

Only with the rise of Protestant theological liberalism did the idea of Mary as virgin mother begin to lose some of the universal support it had enjoyed during the Reformation and long after. In their defense of the verbal inspiration and total inerrancy of the Bible against liberalism, conservative Protestant theologians (e.g., the American Presbyterian fundamentalist J. Gresham Machen, in a book of 1930 entitled *The Virgin Birth of Christ*), to most of whom the development of the doctrine of Mary and even the very notion of any development of doctrine at all seemed abhorrent, nevertheless insisted upon the literal accuracy of all the miracle stories in the Bible, including and especially those dealing with the miraculous conception of Jesus.

Theotokos

The first major theological controversy over Mary had to do with the propriety of applying to her the title of *theotokos*, Bearer of God or, more simply, Mother of God. This was once again a way of discussing language about Mary in order to determine the most appropriate way of believing and teaching about her Son.

One of the earliest reliable instances of the title *theotokos*, but one that serves as evidence for even earlier usage, occurs in the treatise of the emperor Julian ("the Apostate"), *Against the Galileans*: "Why," he asks in annoyance at the Christians whose communion he once shared but had now forsaken, "do you persist in calling Mary *theotokos*?" From the context it is plausible to conclude that Julian was referring chiefly to works not of dogmatics but of devotion and that these were the chief provenance of the title *theotokos*. If, as many scholars believe, the Latin hymn to Mary *Sub tuum praesidium* ("Under your protection") rests upon an earlier Greek original, now lost, that may well have been one of the specific instances of the title of which Julian was thinking. The title itself was, in the eyes of its defenders, an unavoidable implication of the dogma of the full deity of Christ as this was established by the Councils of Nicaea and Constantinople in the fourth century. This dogma was accepted even by the opponents of such a designation for Mary. By the end of the fourth century, therefore, the title had successfully established itself in various sections of the church.

Because it seemed to him that the supporters of the title were guilty of confounding the human and the divine natures of Christ by uniting them in such a way that the authenticity of the former was impaired, the patriarch of Constantinople, Nestorius, objected to its use, preferring the less explicit title *christokos*, "because," he said, "it both removes the blasphemy" of denying the full deity of Christ "and avoids the evil" of compromising the full humanity. Along with other aspects of his teaching, Nestorius's objections were condemned for a mixture of theological, political, and personal reasons by the Council of Ephesus in 431, which met in the great double church of Saint Mary there and decreed that Mary was to be called *theotokos*.

In the devotion of eastern Christendom, the *theotokos* (in Russian, *Bogoroditsa*) has played a major role. Indeed, through most of the history of the development we are describing here, the East has led the way for the West—in devotion, in doctrine, in art. For example, one of the most celebrated of all Roman Catholic images of Mary, the "Miraculous Icon of the Mother of God on the Jasna Góra in Częctochowa," Poland, was probably the work of Greek artists, although the tradition attributes it to Saint Luke and the wood on which it is painted to the carpenter shop of Saint Joseph. The countless icons of the *theotokos* in Greek churches, Serbian monasteries, and (even now) Russian homes are an expression of Eastern devotion to her. Yet under the title of *Mater Dei*, Mother of God, the *theotokos* has had a history of her own in the West as well. As Throne of Wisdom (*Sedes Sapientiae*), she was celebrated in Romanesque sculpture; in such touching sequences as that in the present volume, the story of her earthly life became part of both Christian piety and folk life throughout western Christendom, and her coronation (plate 48) a vindication of her status as Mother of God and Queen of Heaven.

Through its incorporation in the closing words of the *Ave Maria*—"Holy Mary, Mother of God, pray for us sinners, now and in the hour of our death. Amen"—the title Mother of God has circulated throughout western Catholicism. Since its standing as a way of confessing the orthodox doctrine of Christ was indisputable, the statement of the Lutheran Formula of Concord in 1577 echoed the beliefs of many, perhaps most, Protestants of the first and second generation: "We believe, teach, and confess that Mary conceived and bore not a plain, ordinary, mere man but the veritable Son of God; for this reason she is rightly called, and truly is, the Mother of God." It seems fair to say that the title thus assumed a place in the theology, though not equally in the piety or hymnody, of orthodox Protestantism. It is also as Mother of God that the Virgin is termed mediatrix. Through many documents of the popes, including Leo XIII and Pius XII, the official teaching of the church's magisterium has sought to make clear that this latter term is not intended to detract from the glory of Christ as the sole Mediator of reconciliation (1 Tim. 2:5) between God and the human race and that Mary functions as Mediatrix of intercession between Christ and the human race, as she did at Cana in Galilee (John 2:3), represented in plate 33.

Semper Virgo

In the strict sense, all that is asserted in the New Testament is virginal conception rather than virgin birth, but one corollary that could be deduced from the New Testament assertion of Mary's virginity in the conception of Jesus was the doctrine of her perpetual virginity (*Semper virgo*), not only *ante partum* (before birth) but *in partu* (in birth) and *post partum* (after birth), as the phraseology came to stand. The Apostles' Creed appears to teach at least her virginity *in partu* when it says "born of the virgin Mary" rather than, as the Nicene Creed does, "incarnate by the Holy Spirit of the virgin Mary." But, as Philip J. Donnelly has said, "Mary's virginity after the birth of Christ is not contained explicitly in Scripture. . . . This full awareness required a long process of maturation concerning the virgin birth and Mary's virginity after Christ's birth."

Thus the doctrine had no explicit warrant in the New Testament, the earliest mention of it having occurred in the apocryphal *Protogospel of James*. Such Old Testament images as the gate that is shut (*porta clausa*) in Ezekiel 44:2, or the garden locked (*hortus conclusus*) in Song of Solomon 4:12, as expounded by Jerome in his *Against Jovinian*, were probably convincing only to those who already believed the doctrine. The argument that Christ in the Gospel of John (20:19) entered through closed doors, though in a sense only an argument from analogy, could be taken as more, for both this miracle and the virgin birth were possible (though not necessary) implications of his transcendence over the laws of nature, of which he was the sovereign author, not the obedient subject.

In addition, the perpetual virginity posed two problems of biblical interpretation, both of which were discussed in detail by defenders of the doctrine of *Semper virgo* from Jerome to Martin Luther. One was the evident implication of such statements in the Gospels as the one that Mary was found to be with child "before" she and Joseph came together as man and wife (Matt. 1:18) and that they did not come together "until she had borne a son" (Matt. 1:25), or that Jesus was Mary's "first-born son" (Luke 2:7). On the face of it, these statements did seem to imply that Mary must have come together with Joseph after the birth of Jesus and that she seems to have borne additional children. But Luther, speaking here for the consensus of the patristic and medieval tradition, asserted in reply that "the Red Sea fell upon Pharaoh before he came out of it. From this it does not follow that Pharaoh came out of it, when the Red Sea had fallen over him, but that he did not come out of it."

A related problem, already present in the question of the status of Jesus as firstborn, was that of the "brothers" of Jesus. In the Gospel pericope included as Mark 3:31-35, Jesus does point beyond his immediate family to those around him, designating all of them as his "mother" and his "brothers," but that would not seem to negate the family relationship of the "brothers" any more than it does that of the "mother." Elsewhere (Matt. 13:55-56), his fellow citizens at Nazareth not only call him the "carpenter's son" but give the names of his "brothers" and refer to his "sisters" as well. The apostle Paul, too, knew of those who were called "brothers" of the Lord" (1 Cor. 9:5; Gal. 1:19). But defenders of the perpetual virginity, again including both Jerome and Luther, have explained these either as kinsmen or as children of Joseph by a previous marriage or as children of another Mary and of Cleophas. And in Jerome's words, "Every only-begotten son is a firstborn son, but not every firstborn is an only-begotten"; Jesus had been both.

Therefore *Semper virgo* has been seen above all as a fully warranted extension of the biblical doctrine rather than a contradiction of it. Athanasius, writing against the Arians in the fourth century, professed to find a parallel between "denying that the Son is from the Father by nature" and "denying that he took human flesh of Mary Ever-Virgin." Partly because of the biblical problems, however, the identification of Mary as *Semper virgo* has not been supported as broadly across the churches of Christendom as has the doctrine of the virginal conception or even the title *theotokos*, and despite Luther's espousal of it, the number of Lutherans and other Protestants who would make it their own today is probably quite small.

Immaculata

As the image of Mary as *Semper virgo* implied an integral purity of body and soul in her, so, in the opinion of many early theologians, she was free of other sins as well. The conviction that she did not in fact commit any actual sins was widespread among the church fathers. They regularly explained her observance of the rite of purification (Luke 2:22) as occasioned by her obedience to the Mosaic law, not by her need to be purified of sin, and the apparent harshness of the words of Jesus in John 2:4 at the wedding in Cana (plate 33), translated, for example, in the King James Version as "Woman, what have I to do with thee?" was moderated to a more literal and neutral "O woman, what have you to do with me?" in the Revised Standard Version. But they usually did not find it necessary to explain at any length how it was that she was free of sin, only that she was.

It was the development of doctrine in western Christendom that made such an explanation necessary and eventually made it possible. Like most issues in the theology of the Latin West, this one had its roots in the thought of Augustine. It was he who formulated for most of Protestantism, no less than for Roman Catholicism, the doctrine of original sin, according to which the entire human race had through Adam become polluted with the contagion of original sin, which was transmitted as life itself was transmitted, through the sexual union of man and woman. As the Son of the virgin

Mother, without a human father, Jesus Christ had been exempt from this universal rule. But what about his mother?

To this Augustine replied in his treatise *On Nature and Grace*: "We must make an exception of the virgin Mary, concerning whom I wish to raise no question when it touches the subject of sins, out of honor to the Lord [Jesus]. For from him we know what abundance of grace for overcoming sin in every particular was conferred upon her [*quid ei plus gratiae collatum fuerit ad vincendum omni ex parte peccatum*] who merited to conceive and give birth to the One who undoubtedly had no sin." Stamped as it was with the authority of the "doctor of grace" and acknowledged champion of orthodox anthropology, this identification of Mary as an exception, or more precisely as the exception alongside her divine Son, carried great weight.

Ranged against Augustine's statement of Mary as an exception was an epistle of Bernard of Clairvaux, in which he argued on a variety of grounds in opposition to the idea that Mary had been exempt from original sin: there was no liturgical warrant for it; it seemed to contradict the unquestionable teaching of the faith that Christ was the Savior from sin for all human beings, including Mary; and theologically it would seem to necessitate an infinite regress of immaculately conceived ancestors. Bernard did add the stipulation, however, that he would yield to the authority of Rome if the church should speak on the matter. The impasse between the Augustinian and Bernardine theories was resolved when Duns Scotus found a way of teaching that Christ as the perfect Savior of all had saved his mother in the most perfect way possible—by preserving her rather than rescuing her from original sin. That position eventually carried the day, but it did not do so without a millennium of conflict. It was in fact almost exactly a millennium, for Augustine died in 430 and there was no official conciliar declaration of the exceptional status of Mary in relation to original sin until 1439 at the Council of Basel. Because that council was, by that time, technically in schism, its dogmatic decree was not binding, and the official and final resolution of the issue did not come until 1854. In that year Pope Pius IX promulgated the dogma of the Immaculate Conception according to which Mary was not only pure in her life and in her birth, but "at the first instant of her conception was preserved immaculate from all stain of original sin, by the singular grace and privilege granted her by Almighty God"—all of this, however, only "through the merits of Christ Jesus, Savior of mankind."

Assumpta

Bernard's opposition to the doctrine of the Immaculate Conception of Mary did not apply to the doctrine of Assumption, for although it too was lacking in explicit warrant, it did have, and had had for centuries, a place on the church's calendar. Therefore Bernard preached some of his most eloquent Marian sermons on the Feast of the Assumption, and he took it for granted that anyone who would dare to deny the Assumption was a heretic. As plates 47 and 48 show, it was deeply grounded in the piety and in the iconography of Catholic Europe. Yet it did not have the official status of a dogma of the church.

Therefore, as soon as the Immaculate Conception was promulgated in 1854, petitions began coming in to the Vatican for a definition regarding the Assumption of the Virgin into heaven. During the century that followed, more than eight million persons signed such petitions. Yet Rome continued to hesitate. Despite its grounding in piety, liturgy, and art, the Assumption seemed to be utterly devoid of biblical proof, even as a necessary implication from acknowledged teaching (which is what the Immaculate Conception was). At best, there were the analogies of Enoch and of Elijah, who had been taken up into heaven while still living. There was the promise of Jesus in John 14:3, "When I go and prepare a place for you, I will come again and take you to myself, that where I am you may be also," which seemed to apply in some special way to Mary. And there was the *argumentum e silentio*, the argument from silence, but a powerful argument nonetheless: If relics from the bodies of lesser saints had performed miracles, should there not have been miracles attributed to relics of her body? And yet no miracles and no relics had been authenticated.

But all such arguments seemed to be insufficient to establish a dogma, and on the positive side even the earliest doctrinal and liturgical tradition had appeared relatively late in history. Finally, Pope Pius XII made the dogma official in 1950, drawing together several of the titles we have been analyzing here and declaring "that the immaculate Mother of God, Mary *Semper virgo*, when the course of her earthly life was run, was assumed in body and soul to heavenly glory." Plate 46, depicting the death of Mary—or, to use the common euphemism, her "dormiton" (in Greek, *koimēsis*)—raises a question not addressed in Pope Pius's *Munificentissimus Deus*: Did Mary die? The majority of orthodox teachers had said that she did, some said that she did not, and some inclined to the view that she died but was immediately resurrected. Although there was some opposition to the "new" dogma from the non-Catholic world (the Protestants attacking it as unscriptural and the Eastern Orthodox attacking it as unauthorized though probably true), it did not remain at the center of attention for long. For the announcement of the Second Vatican Council less than a decade later put most such questions aside, and the council itself did not make any new declarations about Mary, preferring to stress her place as archetype of the church and, above all, to reaffirm her close identification with her Son: plate 48 makes clear that Mary is Queen but that she receives her status as Queen from Christ, who is King of kings.

In addition to bearing these official titles and roles assigned to her by Catholic Christianity, the Virgin (as the plants and animals in these plates suggest) has served to symbolize the redemption of the total life of the natural world and thereby to provide a bridge between Christianity and those religions of nature that have spoken of this redemption. In the secular life and literature of the West since the days of the German *Minnesänger* and the Provençal troubadours, she has symbolized the nobility of woman. Even those Protestant churches that have most vigorously criticized the Mariolatry they claimed to find in the dogmas of the Immaculate Conception and the Assumption have frequently addressed praises to her in their hymnody that they would have hesitated to express in the prose of their dogmatic theology, calling her (in the familiar hymn

"Ye Watchers and Ye Holy Ones") "higher than the cherubim, more glorious than the seraphim." Thus, in ways Mary could never have anticipated, the words of the *Magnificat* have continued to be fulfilled: "*Ecce enim ex hoc beatam me dicent omnes generationes.*"

Mary and Catholic Practice

Justin Lang, O.F.M.

Is the Marian age of the Catholic church at an end? The Second Vatican Council was theologically astute in formulating the connection between the reality of Mary and the vocation of the church. But in spite of this and in spite of the proclamation of Mary as Queen in 1954 and of "Mary, Mother of the church" in 1964, it seems that even the example of the present pope, John Paul II, is unable to retrieve the strength and spiritual disposition of the devotion to Mary that so conspicuously characterized the life of the church from the beginning of the last century until 1950. This is certainly an irreplaceable loss. But it is also an opportunity.

Those Who Love Always Exaggerate

Catholic theologians can be divided into Mariological maximalists and minimalists. This is very interesting for the reason that in no other field of theology is there a similarly precise and real separation of spirits. At least it is not talked about. But when it comes to Mary, one knows at the outset whose standard bears the old maxim "*De Maria numquam satis*" ("In Mary's regard there is never enough praise") and who would sooner "take leave of Mary." In the magisterial structure of the Catholic church, the tract on Mary is not simply one among others. And Marian piety is also not simply another form of devotion in the life of the Catholic church. Both demonstrate a preparedness for battle, as would seem appropriate for what is in the service of Notre Dame. In a way similar to Mary, the pope is also not simply representative of what is Catholic, even though this may sometimes appear to be the case to the superficial observer.

No, in Catholic thinking, Mary is not entrusted with one or the other function but is the summation of all that the church and Christian life must be if they wish to correspond to their own center, which is called Jesus Christ. Seen from this point of view, there can really only be a maximalist in the Mariological and Marian arena, for the measure of love is always the measureless. And Mary not only fulfilled this measure since she is "full of grace," she also requires this measure of self-sacrifice to the will of the Almighty from the church and from everyone who does her honor. And this did not first occur with Lourdes or Fatima.

Yet the concern of the minimalists should not simply be dismissed, namely, that the human heart is not without its intrigues. And it could easily happen that Mary is so persistently praised in order that the ones praising might themselves be relieved a bit of their own responsibility. And there, where Mary is pressed into the role of privy councillor whose duty it is to clarify various matters of importance for the attentive people of God, there I also no longer recognize the Mother of Good Counsel. Her counsel was so surpassingly good, because it could be stated, "Do everything that he tells you!" (John 2:5). But wherever those who honor Mary are criticized because their hymns are too loud and too long and wherever they are decried as sentimental because of the veneration with which they honor the image of the highly favored one, it is there that I want to listen. For those who love always and necessarily exaggerate. And the veneration of Mary is either a matter of love or a matter of suspicious and exaggerated zeal. For that reason, it is not so terribly important how one expresses one's love for the mother of the Lord. The only thing that is important is the believing heart that beats responsively to the same God as the heart of Mary.

Blessing of Heaven and Earth

What crests in various waves or attracts in hurried reflections is only the surface of the deep waters of the devotion to Mary. Underneath it is quiet and deep, and no one is able to reach the source of this powerful stream. On the shores of these waters the Marian cathedrals and places of pilgrimage grew up. The murmur of the stream's waters keeps the praying of the rosary alive and causes the Ave bells to resound in human souls. The fine and ancient sources of the Catholic devotion to Mary do not spring forth from the studies of those learned in the things of God nor from the headquarters of the Marian societies. Chosen according to the eternal plan of God, Mary is not only the new Eve who fulfilled the oldest desire of humanity. She is also the victorious conqueror and the heir of the ancient mother goddesses who once controlled the ancient Orient. A hymn has been preserved concerning Irnin, the predecessor of the Babylonian Ishtar: "My father gave me the heavens; he gave me the earth. I am the mistress of heaven. The heavens he set on my head like a crown. He placed the earth like a sandal on my foot. The brilliant cloak of the gods he placed around me and handed me the radiant scepter" (H. Uhlig, *Die Sumerer* [Munich, 1976], 120).

When in almost similar fashion Catholic hymns praise Mary, "the most beautiful of all," this is certainly not in the tradition of the mother goddesses of the land of two rivers but in the faith tradition of Revelation 12. The image of the woman of the apocalypse is not some sort of bizarre creation of the human imagination but stands in exact correspondence to the landscape of the human soul, as it also does to the ancient relation between heaven and earth. Jesus Christ speaks of this with all possible clarity when he says (Matt. 5:17) that he has not come in order to abolish and do away with, but to fulfill and complete, everything that without him was condemned to final frustration. He leads it out of the twilight of its former lack of wholeness and he brings it into the full light that he himself is.

This gathering and saving gesture of Christ emerges in the Catholic church in a wealth of expression, which may be confusing for the outsider. In reality, however, the entire multiformity in Christ is ordered according to a new cosmos of redeemed humanity in which Mary also receives a privileged but clearly circumscribed place. The possibility of worshipping Mary does not seriously come to the mind of even the simplest Catholic. But even the most educated theologian cannot ignore her on a daily basis. He would be shocked into reality by the very title of God-bearer (*theotokos*) that was attributed to the girl from Israel by the council held in Ephesus, of all places, where Artemis was honored through the centuries as *magna mater*. Mary does not come to us as a goddess from out of the ancient world's melting pot of religious views and intuitions, though, but as the servant of the Lord and the primordial model of faith. For this reason, Mary could image completely the thematic of fruitful motherhood and splendid virginity, and completely without compromise. Although she was to the same extent fruitful mother and a virgin dedicated to God—in a way that was not conceivable to the pre-Christian understanding—she does not appropriate anything to herself that was not already hers because of her most personal election. She is the bodily image of grace.

At the root of the Catholic devotion to Mary one should take note of the power of this devotion for clarifying the structures of our reality, and especially how the old idols and patterns of yearning evaporate in the light of the sun of Christ and arise to a new life in the Logos, the Son whom God has made "heir of all things" (Heb. 1:2). In line with this clarifying function, all those joys and pains accrue to Mary that are connected with the ideals of bridal love and motherhood. From now on, she is the one who is associated with the longing for protection and veneration that grips humanity in the face of those primordial experiences we articulate in the images of mother and bride. Without this coupling of a unique salvific-historical vocation and the most universal experience of human beings, that religious vitality in which Mary meets the Catholic Christian as the humble handmaiden and as the Queen of heaven, as the one whose life is riddled with pain and filled with joy, as the eternal woman, is not to be comprehended.

Contours of the Doctrinal Formulation

Although her importance is utterly directed toward Christ and although she receives her salvific-historical significance and uniqueness from him alone, Mary nevertheless stands in a characteristic unity of tension with her Son. From the point of view of humanity, it is as if she is the forward position in which created humanity advances into the boundless sea of the God become man. She had to be more deeply entrusted with the incomprehensible center of our salvation. She had to have achieved, in purer and holier fashion than usual, intimate association with that to which she had given the best—that which human beings and God can give each other, life and love. For that reason, it rings somewhat foreign to our sense of life when, in view of the relatively infrequent mentions of Mary in the New Testament, the consequent doctrinal developments of the Marian reality are faulted as being disproportionate or exaggerated.

What was a faith seeking understanding to do when it ever further directed its attention to her in order more deeply to comprehend the reality of Christ? Given the absolutely central proclamation of Christ in the New Testament as the very fulfillment of the will of the Father for humanity, even the smallest mention of the person of Mary was most significant and had to direct the attention of all to her who was so incomprehensibly close and inwardly connected to him as only a mother can be in relation to her child. And there is also the added fact that Mary was never simply thought of as a private person but, in the best biblical tradition, as a representative personality. Her reality qualifies and redefines the meaning of every salvific-historical typology and parallelism (AVE EVA). For this reason, her person and her destiny are intimately connected both with the person and mission of her Son and with our own destiny.

In the face of this highly explosive mixture of faith in Christ and thoughts on the essence of reality, of individuality and social unity, and of the promise-fulfillment tension, the statements of the New Testament with regard to Mary have the function of a spark that is sufficient to ignite the great fire of enthusiasm that has glowed now for two thousand years around her image. The fact that the four great Marian dogmas of the motherhood of God, the perpetual virginity, the Immaculate Conception, and the assumption into heaven are significant in the entire expanse of the history of dogma is a very clear indication that the Marian truth is a point of convergence of the most diverse strains of thought in Christianity.

It is common knowledge that the intellectual presuppositions for the definition of 1854 were developed by the Franciscan Duns Scotus (d. 1308) within the framework of a broad Christocentrism. The development of this context guarded against a double misunderstanding. First of all, it is not as if the two definitions of the ancient church and the two modern dogmas of 1854 and 1905 stand disconnected from each other at the beginning and the end of the prevailing dogmatic development. It is closer to the truth to say that in between there was an extremely intense theological grappling with the mystery of Mary. And second, it is not as if the two dogmas on the motherhood of God and the perpetual virginity arose in close connection with the christological controversies while the two modern Mariological dogmas appear out of nowhere.

Once again, it is closer to the truth to say that the threads that once wove together the ancient church's image of Christ and his virgin mother continue to run through all the following centuries. And it is only by force of this continuity that the modern Mariological developments were able to emerge clearly in the picture of Mary. Only by a comprehensive treatment of all aspects of the Marian reality could those fundamental elements and theological conclusions be developed that in turn established the foundation for the doctrine of these unique privileges of Mary.

"And Splendidly the Air"

During the course of this doctrinal development, not only is the entire "biography" of Mary brought into play, but the outer limits of Roman Catholic doctrinal proclamation are also reached. The further expansion of the Marian mystery occurs in the more appropriate development of feasts and celebrations dedicated to the reality of Mary. Feasts are always the most effective form of making religious truths concrete. As nowhere else, the most varied small streams flow into the feasts. Theological truth and religious intuition, the pain of existence and joyful hope, the poetry of God and nameless longing—these are the streams that move through life and nourish it with eternity.

All of this comes punctually together when summer slowly exhausts itself and August 15 appears on the calendar. There can be no doubt that this ancient Marian celebration of the assumption of Mary into heaven is the feast of our beloved Lady par excellence. Neither the Feast of Mary the Mother of God on January 1, within the octave of Christmas, nor the Feast of the Immaculate Conception on December 8 can so transform their theological preeminence into festive joy that they could displace August 15 as the leading Marian feast.

Anyone who has celebrated this great day of our Lady through the years knows that it does not simply concern the articulation of a dogmatic truth. A sense of painful departure, which is signaled by the gossamers and the harvested fields, also comes into play. What Vatican II teaches is also the faith of the people: "In the interim, just as the Mother of Jesus, glorified in body and soul in heaven, is the image and beginning of the Church as it is to be perfected in the world to come, so too does she shine forth on earth until the coming of the Day of the Lord, as a sign of sure hope and solace to the people of God during its sojourn on earth" (*Luman Gentium*, 68). But the people do not want simply to hear a statement of this belief, they want to experience it in festive liturgy and to smell it in the scent of the blessed baskets of fruits and vegetables. The last of the sparrows as well as the fine haze that somewhat disappears only during midday also belong to this feast.

With the new ordering of the church year in 1969, the Marian feasts and celebrations were also rearranged and divided into three categories. There are first of all the four solemn feasts (January 1, March 25, August 15, and December 8). Next follow the two feasts days of the visitation of Mary (July 2) and the birth of Mary (September 8). And finally there are nine memorial days. Our Lady of Lourdes (February 11), Our Lady of Mount Carmel (July 16), the Dedication of the Basilica of Saint Mary Major (August 5), the Queenship of Mary (August 22), the Name of Mary (September 12), Our Lady of Sorrows (September 15), Our Lady of the Rosary (October 7), the Presentation of Mary (November 21), and the Immaculate Heart of Mary (the Saturday after the second Sunday after Pentecost).

This is a well-ordered assemblage with well-founded distinctions in importance. But when one looks at the various customs of the people, it is difficult to see how the real worth of these days comes to expression in the hierarchical ranking. From one area to another, from one Marian venerator to another, there exist highly individual preferences based on fairly obscure criteria. Apart from August 15, whose leading position is presumably nowhere challenged, the most varied constellations are possible. Quite often to be found in the forefront is the Presentation of the Lord (February 2), which is no longer a Marian feast (it was formerly the Feast of the Purification of Mary, or Candlemas Day). A similar pride of place is given to the Birth of Mary (September 8) and the no longer observed Friday of Sorrows, with its unforgettable Stabat Mater ("At the cross, her station keeping").

If we add the season of Advent with its pervasive Marian atmosphere, plus the month of May, strangely laden with sentiment, as well as October, the month of the rosary, then it is easy to see how the Marian venerators actually never have to wait long for the next impulse for their devotion. If they further see how these feasts have as pivot points moments from the life of Christ that connect not only January 1 but also February 2 and March 25—the Annunciation of Mary—with Christmas, then they will soon understand why the visitation of Mary is celebrated on July 2 and the Queenship of Mary on August 22. The Marian days establish a certain familiarity with the "holy network of relations."

For this reason, no one insists that on these days every sentence of a prayer or of a sermon explicitly mention the contextual connection of the Marian celebration with Christ. The connection is always presumed.

Even without more advanced historical-liturgical studies, which are admittedly very interesting, these celebrations and memorials fulfill the spirit of what Vatican II had in mind when it wrote, "In celebrating this annual cycle of Christ's mysteries, holy Church honors with special love the Blessed Mary, Mother of God, who is joined by an inseparable bond to the saving work of her Son. In her the Church holds up and admires the most excellent fruit of the redemption, and joyfully contemplates, as in a faultless model, that which she herself wholly desires and hopes to be" (*Sacrosanctum Concilium*, 103).

Sing and Proclaim All Days

The fundamental liturgical structures of the Marian feasts communicate first of all an atmosphere that mystically envelops the venerator of Mary. And the prayers and hymns of these feasts attempt to articulate further this specifically Marian sense of life. There exists here a characteristic dialectic between a verbal and melodius exuberance and a blissful movement into silence. The famous *Hymnos akathistos*, for example, allows the entire height and depth of the Marian mystery to shine forth in ever new cascades of words, as we can observe in the following lines:

Hail, Mother of the most holy star;
hail, Morning light of the mystical life.
Hail, you who extinguish smoldering error;
hail, you who show their majesty to all consecrated to the Trinity.

Hail, you who drive away brutality and inhumanity;
hail, in Christ we see the friend of humanity as Lord.

Hail, you who free us from pagan worship;
hail, you who preserve us from the offspring of discord.
Hail, you who put an end to the worship of fire;
hail, you who free those obsessed with greed.
Hail, you who show the faithful the path of Wisdom;
hail, you who fill al creatures with bliss.

Hail, you virgin Mother!

On the other hand, the no less famous poet Paul Claudel wishes to say nothing to or about Mary when he confesses:

At midday I see the church open,
It draws me within.
I come, Mother of Jesus Christ,
Not to pray.
I have nothing to bring you,
Or to ask of you.
I only come, O Mother,
To gaze at you,
To see you, to cry simply out of joy,
Because I know that I am your child,
And that you are there. . . .

With these words the poet brings to expression an utterly decisive moment of the Catholic devotion to Mary—simply to dwell in the movement of this holy life; to experience the healing power of the purity and benevolent understanding; on the road to one's destination to be already a little at home.

In no century is there a dearth of prayers and hymns. Even to this day some of these are recited or sung, but for the most part they have become components of a rather vast anthology. Many of these items must be sung in order that the full richness of religious emotion and passionate devotion that they contain may be experienced. This is principally true of the Marian antiphons that conclude the church's Office of the Hours. And these cannot without consequence be deprived of their Latin linguistic finery, in which alone the full value of their unmistakable mixture of inwardness and precision comes to expression: "*Salve Regina, mater misericordiae*" ("Hail, holy Queen, mother of mercy"); "*alma redemptoris mater*" ("nurturing Mother of our Redeemer"); "*Regina caeli, laetare*" ("Queen of heaven, rejoice").

These antiphonal melodies have become such an integral part of the solemn feasts and different seasons of the church year that they automatically swell into the hearts and minds and flow from the lips of the Catholic worshipper. Mary appears in them as an entirely self-evident and in some way necessary ingredient of the church's life. With few words the fundamental importance of Mary to us is regularly recalled.

Similar accents are set by the other ancient Marian prayers of common usage, of which naturally the *Magnificat* ("My soul proclaims the greatness of the Lord") holds pride of place. This prayer is actually the prayer of Mary herself, which the church now makes its own. But the oldest Marian prayer, which begins with the words "*Sub tuum praesidium*" ("Under your protection") does not long sustain the posture of exaggerated courtesy but comes immediately to the point:

> We flee to your protection, O holy Mother of God. In our needs do not disdain our prayer, but save us at all times from all dangers, O glorious and favored Virgin, our Lady, our Mediatrix, our Advocate. Lead us to your Son; commend us to your Son; present us to your Son.

A similar understanding and emotion is to be found in the "Hail, Mary" ("*Ave Maria*") or in the popular prayer of Bernard of Clairvaux "Remember, most loving virgin Mary"

(*Memorare*). None of our modern skepticism can infect the clear knowledge of salvation that allures in these brief and colorful prayers. Everything is fundamentally clear. The one praying knows who Mary is and who her Son is. One knows that one is a sinner, that our life in the world is not a harmless game, and that God is Father. One knows the way and the destination. Thus one's prayer with the two moments in view that especially matter: "Holy, Mary, Mother of God, pray for us sinners, now and at the hour of our death!"

The rosary, the Angelus, and also the Litany of Loretto expand on these basic Marian prayers. Remaining within the sphere of this simple world of faith, they demonstrate, however, a higher level of specialization. The Angelus, for instance, prayed in the morning, at noon, and in the evening, intends to embed the moment of the Incarnation into every hour of our time. In this way, it constantly and newly strengthens the ties between time and eternity.

In like manner, the rosary is of importance in making use of the *Ave Maria* for meditation purposes. In connection with the rosary, a totally new function accrues to this primordial Marian prayer. It is not the content of the prayer that stands in the forefront, but rather its capacity for being a means of flowing beyond oneself into the mysteries of the incarnation, of the suffering and glorification of Christ in the Spirit, which are considered in connection with Mary. The Litany of Loretto, on the other hand, is a roughly and simply constructed prayer that takes up the concerns of the *hymnos akathistos* in the more sober language of Rome. The few flights of lyrical fancy remain precious ornamentation, which does not develop into any thematic of its own.

And what of the incalculable number of hymns that are the favorites at the Marian devotions, on pilgrimages, for the religious consecrations of our lives, and at the special novenas? Because chaff and wheat are brought together in these situations in an easy harmony, one must proceed critically with what is offered. But it is entirely worth the effort. In the midst of unrestrained effusions or purse-lipped complaints or accusations, there is a good deal of the praise of Mary that is popular but also of a high religious quality. Thus all can presumably lend themselves to the spirit of the piece when they hear sung:

Mary, my intention is to love you at all times,
you were granted the fullness of grace:
upon you, Virgin, the Spirit descended,
you, Mother, have gifted us with the Savior.

The precise way in which popular Marian piety knows how to connect Christian belief with a valuable appreciation of the religious quality of nature is always impressive. In doing this, it maintains for the life of the church that warmth and delight that it needs.

In a Thousand Images

The image plays a much greater role in the Catholic devotion to Mary than does the word. In contrast to the thinking of Protestant Christianity, which is based more on hearing, the Catholic church has always been the home of the thinking that favors sight. In this the Catholic church has been entirely faithful to Jesus Christ, who always spoke in images and parables and left nothing untouched by vividness and powerful colors. In contrast to the thinking based on hearing, the thinking based on sight is not discursive but is an integrating power. It has the totality of its object in view, of which, to be sure, individual details can be recognized, but details that flow into and mutually clarify and develop each other. For that reason, the many images we have of Mary do not exclude, but, on the contrary, incorporate one another.

And this is not only self-evident with regard to the images we have around us but is primarily true of the images within us. Thinking in images always sets free an entire world of images in which the individual images always represent the whole. The various madonnas that beautify the fountains, the gables, the wayside shrines of the Main-Frankish villages, for instance, not only are not in competition with each other but are together fundamental for the atmosphere and tone of the Catholic Marian belief. And it is precisely at this point that images demonstrate that they are images. For when one is taken on its own, it is not sufficient to depict the intended reality so accurately that every further image would have to be considered artificial by comparison since the one was already perfectly expressive of that reality.

Two important facts of the Catholic devotion to Mary are connected with this function of the image: legends and portraits. And they always occasion a concerned inquiry. There is, first of all, the familiar phenomenon of the creation of legends from out of the residue of hagiography. There are an endless number of Marian legends that can ignite on the occasion of all sorts of events and extraordinary happenings. Fundamentally, all that is light and pure; reserved but at the same time translucent; blue and fragrant; precious and hidden—all of these hint of Mary. The Middle Ages made whole segments of the plant and animals kingdoms exclusively symbolic of Mary and scarcely any one of these symbols was without an enchanting legend that clarified the connection with her.

It is only when the symbol is reshaped within a functioning and an occasion that it loses its ambiguity and can be authentic in what it claims to communicate. This is the case, for instance, with the bindweed, whose blossom has an unmistakable similarity to the cup of a drinking vessel. But it became known as the little glass of the Mother of God for the following reason:

One day a driver got stuck with his wagon, which was heavily laden with wine. He could not budge from the spot. The Mother of God of the Road came along and saw that the poor man was in trouble and she spoke to him: "I am tired and thirsty; give me a glass of wine." The driver answered: "Gladly, but I have no glass within which I could give you the wine." Thereupon the Mother of God broke off a small white blossom with red stripes. The driver filled the blossom with wine and the Mother of God drank it. And at that moment the wagon was free and the driver could travel on. But the blossom is called to this day "the little glass of the Mother of God." (The Brothers Grimm)

If, on the one hand, the incentive for the creation of legends clearly comes from the overflow of a heart that desires to pour itself out into the wide world of concrete manifestations, so, on the other hand, do the much discussed appearances of Mary (at least where they are considered to be authentic) somehow have their incentive in Mary herself or in God with whom she dwells. But the point is that even here the function of the image cannot be dispensed with. Even with authentic visions and appearances, we are confronted in a definite sense with imagination or the power of imaging. What shows itself to the visionary is not Mary as such but an image of her that so shines up in this or that garment, at one time laughing and at another time crying, that it seems as if this were actually taking place in the external world. In reality it is a question of an "imaginative vision" (K. Rahner) that is, as it were, a sensual reaction to an influence of God that for its part is more spiritual and personal and also far less perceptible than the sensual image it arouses. The observed image is, in the deepest and most authentic vision, also always seen through the lens of the one to whom it appears. And it would be meaningless in this situation to want to pit divine influence and human receptivity against each other. With regard to the question of authenticity, we must finally attend to the warning of Jesus: "You will know them by their fruits" (Matt. 7:16).

Along with these internal images, the portraits that Christian art has created of Mary present a world of external images that are accessible to everyone who has eyes to perceive the beauty. After 431, Mary became an autonomous theme for art. This quickly developed in the East into a restricted canon of image types, whereas in the west the development was much freer: the Mother of God, the Enthroned (Maesta), the Mother of Mercy, the Beautiful Madonna, the Mother of Sorrows (Pietà), the Queen of Heaven. Each one of these image types developed in unbounded fashion into connections with religious representations, artistic traditions, and local specialties. With the help of two apocryphal writings, the *Protogospel of James* (second century) and the *Gospel of Pseudo-Matthew* (fifth century), the large gaps the New Testament left open with regard to the ancestry and early years of Mary could be filled in. The image sequence of the life of Mary is in its foundation the creation of a typically popular piety. But this piety scarcely contributed less than the great cult and devotional portraits of Mary to those thoughtful words of Plotinus that have been fulfilled in the Catholic church: "In their beholding the souls are and become that upon which they gave" (*Enneads* V.8).

Illustration Acknowledgments

plates 1, 3–5, 12, 14, 17–23, 26, 30, 33, 48   Buxtehuder Altar, Master Bertram of Minden (c. 1345–c.1415). Photos © Hamburg Kunsthalle/Bridgeman Art Library. Used by permission.

plate 2   Desert of Judah, Israel. Photo © Erich Lessing/Art Resource, NY. Used by permission.

plate 6   Antependium: scenes from the life of the Virgin. From the church of Thornham Parva. Detail of a panel: The Education of the Virgin. Painted on wood. 14th century. Photo: Gérard Blot. Musée du Moyen Âge (Cluny), Paris, France. Photo © Réunion des Musées Nationaux/Art Resource, NY.

plate 8   Steps leading to a platform at the west wall of the Temple Mount of Jerusalem, Israel. Photo © Erich Lessing/Art Resource, NY. Used by permission.

plates 9, 11, 37–42, 44, 46   Monks' Altar of Göttingen and the Golden Panel of Lüneburg: Photos © Niedersächsisches Landesmuseum, Hannover. Used by permission.

plates 10, 15   Musée de l'œuvre Notre Dame de Strasbourg. Photo © A. Plisson. Used by permission.

plate 13   Photo © Israelimages/Douglas Guthrie. Used by permission.

plates 16, 25, 27, 31–32, 34–36, 43   © Corel Corporation. Used by permission.

plate 24   Gentile da Fabriano (1385–1427). Madonna and Child. Museo di S. Matteo, Pisa, Italy. Photo © Scala/Art Resource, NY. Used by permission.

plate 28   The return from Egypt to Nazareth. Hora Church (Kariye Camii), Istanbul, Turkey. Photo © Erich Lessing/Art Resource, NY. Used by permission.

plate 29   The Old Roman Road from Jericho to Jerusalem, built in the era of Emperor Hadrian. Photo © Erich Lessing/Art Resource, NY. Used by permission.

plate 45   Entrance into one of the slope-houses (*Bueldueldag*) along the stairway. First to sixth century CE. Ephesus, Turkey. Photo © Erich Lessing/Art Resource. Used by permission.

plate 47   Benozzo Gozzoli (1420–1497). Madonna presenting the sash to Saint Thomas. Predella: Life of the Virgin Mary. Pinacoteca, Vatican Museum, Vatican State. Photo © Scala/Art Resource, NY. Used by permission.